CONDOR LEGION
The Wehrmacht's Training Ground

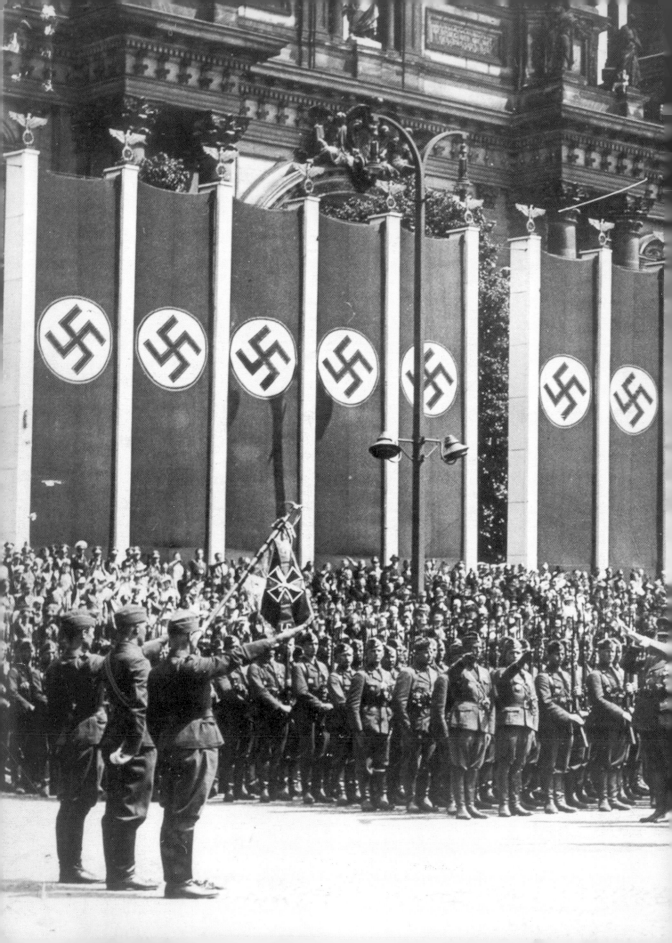

SPEARHEAD

CONDOR LEGION
The Wehrmacht's Training Ground

Ian Westwell

Ian Allan
PUBLISHING

Acknowledgements

Editor: Phil Kelly
Design: Compendium design
Maps and artwork: Mark Franklin
Photos: As credited. Thanks to TRH Pictures, Chris Ellis, Austin Brown, Jak Mallmann-Showell and Brian L. Davies.

Note: Internet site information provided in the Reference section was correct when provided by the author. The publisher can accept no responsibility for this information becoming incorrect.

Previous Pages: Hitler saluting the Special Colour for the Legion Condor on 6 June 1939 during the victory parade in Berlin.

First published 2004

ISBN 0 7110 3043 X

Published by Ian Allan Publishing Ltd

an imprint of Ian Allan Publishing Ltd, Hersham, Surrey KT12 4RG
Printed in England by Ian Allan Printing Ltd, Hersham, Surrey KT12 4RG

Code: 0410/B

British Library Cataloguing in Publication Data
A CIP catalogue record for this book is available from the British Library

Ranks of the Condor Legion

German	Spanish equivalent
General	
Oberst	Coronel
Oberstleutnant	Teniente Coronel
Comandante	Major
Hauptmann	Capitán
Oberleutnant	
Leutnant	Leniente
Oberfeldwebel	Alférez
Feldwebel	
Unteroffizier	Suboficial
Legionär	Cabo

The Participants

Accion Española Monarchist party
Accion Popular Catholic party, later a part of Confederacion Espanola de Derechas Autonomas

Bloque Obrero Y Campesino (BOC) Communist group with links to Partido Obrero de Unificación Marxista

Camisa Azul The 'Blue Shirts'. Irish fascists fighting with the republicans
Carlismo Monarchists

Confederación Española de Derechas Autónomas (CEDA) Catholic party
Confederación Nacional de Trabajo (CNT) Anarcho-Syndicalist trade union
Esquerra Republicana de Catalunya (ERC) Catalan socialist party

Falange Española Fascist Party, later a part of Falange Española Tradicionalista y de las Juntas de Ofensiva Nacional-Sindicalista
Falange Española de la JONS see Falange Española Tradicionalista y de las Juntas de Ofensiva Nacional-Sindicalista
Falange Española Tradicionalista y de las Juntas de Ofensiva Nacional-Sindicalista (FET) Fascist party founded in 1937 when Falange Española Tradicionalista and Juntas de Ofensiva Nacional-Sindicalista merged
Federación Anarquista Ibérica (FAI) Federation of anarchist groups in Spain and Portugal
Federación de Juventudes Socialistas (FJS) Socialist youth organisation, later a part of Juventudes Socialistas Unificadas
Federación Ibérica de Juventudes Libertarias (FIJL) Anarchist youth organisation

International Brigades Units made up of foreign volunteers fighting for the republicans
Izquierda Comunista Communist party, later a part of Partido Obrero de Unificación Marxista
Izquierda Republicana Republican socialist party

Juventud Comunista Ibérica (JCI) Youth organisation of Partido Obrero de Unificación Marxistas
Juventud de Acción Popular (JAP) Catholic youth organisation
Juntas de Ofensiva Nacional-Sindicalista (JONS) Fascist Party, later a part of Falange Española Tradicionalista y de las Juntas de Ofensiva Nacional-Sindicalista
Juventudes Socialistas Unificadas (JSU) Socialist youth organisation

Lojalists See republican
Los Amigos de Durruti Anarchist opposition group within the CNT, FAI and FIJL

Margaritas Monarchist women's organisation
Mujeres Libres Anarchist women's organisation

CONTENTS

Nationalists Those fighting against the government led by Franco

Partido Agrario Catholic party, later a part of Confederacion Espanola de Derechas Autonomas

Partido Communista de Espana (PCE) Pro-Soviet Communist Party

Partido Nacionalista Vasco (PNV) Basque separatist party

Partido Obrero de Unificación Marxista (POUM) Anti-Soviet Communist party

Partido Republicano Radical Republican socialist party

Partido Socialista Unificado de Cataluña (PSUC) Catalan Pro-Soviet Communist Party

Partit Comunista Catalá Catalan Communist Party

Pelayos Monarchist youth organisation

Renovacion Española Monarchist party

Republicans Those fighting for the government against Franco's Nationalists

Requetes Monarchist military

Servicio Investigacion Militar (SIM) Political police force controlled by the pro-Soviet communists

Unión General de Trabajadores (UGT) Socialist trade union

Unión Militar Española (UME) Conservative officers group

Unión Militar Republicana Antifascista (UMRA) Republican officers group

Unión Republicana Republican socialist party

ORIGINS & HISTORY

The outbreak of the Spanish Civil War in 1936 was the result of long-term political imbalances within a country that was traditionally ruled by a conservative, pro-monarchy elite of large landowners allied to the military and Catholic Church. The masses, the impoverished rural farm labourers and the growing numbers of the city-dwelling industrial working class, had few rights with little access to land, education or health care. Their clamour for social, economic and political reform—anathema to the ruling class but a central tenet of Spain's various left-wing factions who had been inspired in part by the recent Communist take-over of Russia—grew steadily stronger and led to violent unrest in the early 1920s. This provoked a backlash from the conservatives and traditionalists led by the military and in 1923 General Miguel Primo de Rivera seized power with the authority of King Alfonso XIII and suspended the country's constitution. Order was imposed from above but nothing was done to address Spain's deep-lying problems and it was eight years before the first move to reintroduce the constitution was made.

FOUNDING THE SECOND REPUBLIC

In April 1931 the people of Spain were permitted to vote in municipal elections. Although pro-monarchists candidates enjoyed more success than their opponents, the king and his closest supporters recognised that where the results really counted, in the country's larger towns and cities, the anti-monarchist parties of the left had enjoyed overwhelming support. Alfonso abdicated, probably forestalling an immediate descent into civil war, and on April 14 the Second Republic was proclaimed against a background of high expectation among the poor and considerable foreboding among the traditionalists. The new leadership of the Provisional Government faced one almost intractable problem— how to satisfy the working class's demand for rapid wide-ranging reform without further alienating the still-powerful but disgruntled traditionalists. A general election in June confirmed the growing strength of the Spanish left but the new government was a loose coalition containing a sizeable number of left-wing parties, such as the Spanish Socialist Workers' Party, while the defeated traditionalist alliance contained two reactionary pro-monarchists groups, the Alfonsists and the Carlists. What was lacking was a broad-based centre party to balance the extremists of both left and right. The question of political stability was never resolved and, against a background of growing unrest from both the extreme left and right, Spain staggered from one crisis to another. As the government debated and slowly implemented some reformist legislation during 1932, the Anarchists, a powerful political grouping that refused to enter the mainstream political arena, sponsored strikes in January that resulted in considerable bloodshed while General José Sanjurjo launched an unsuccessful right-wing coup in August. Large sections of the working class blamed the government for using repressive measures reminiscent of the

Above: A young Franco: he would rule Spain from the end of the Civil War until his death 1975. *TRH Pictures*

old regime to contain the disorder while the right complained that it was incapable of restoring the rule of law.

The coalition government gradually disintegrated over the following year and fresh elections were held in November 1933. Two parties fought the contest with realistic hopes of victory: the Spanish Socialist Workers' Party, standing on a ticket of further but generally watered-down reform, was opposed by CEDA, the Spanish Confederation of right-wing groups formed the previous February, which sought a return to a more traditionalist Spain and was allied with some of the monarchists and the Radicals, a centrist group. Due to a quirk of Spanish voting system, the fractured nature of left-wing politics and the decision of the Anarchists to abstain from the election, CEDA and the Radicals won overwhelmingly and began repealing much of the previous government's progressive legislation. Seeing a return to the repressive era from before the Second Republic and a swift end to Spain's experiment with democracy, elements of the left abandoned parliament and took direct action in October 1934. There were uprisings in Madrid and Barcelona as well as strikes across the country, all of which were put down with considerable loss of life. Along the northern coast, General Francisco Franco y Bahamonde led regular units of the Spanish Foreign Legion and Moroccan troops, normally stationed in Spanish Morocco, against the Basques, who had proclaimed an autonomous Socialist Republic, and killed around 1,000 locals in a brutal campaign of repression that was followed by the imprisonment and deportation of many thousands. These clashes further hardened the country's deep political divisions and made civil war almost inevitable; those on the radical left increasingly believed that parliamentary democracy was a sham, while to many on the far right the recent events indicated that order could only be restored through force. Although the government survived the uprisings, its legitimacy had been undermined and it collapsed completely in 1935, when the Radicals were implicated in a corruption scandal.

THE OUTBREAK OF CIVIL WAR

New elections were arranged for 16 February 1936, although many on both the extreme left and right had by then abandoned the ballot box; on hearing of the forthcoming election a cabal of generals contemplated a coup but stayed their hand at the last minute. When the results were announced the Popular Front, a left-wing alliance, gained 280 seats in parliament out of 470; CEDA won just 87. To many on the right it seemed that regaining power via the ballot box was no longer a practical proposition. However, the Popular Front's landslide victory did not bring stability and waves of unrest swept the Spanish countryside and cities. In rural areas, particularly in the conservative south and west, impoverished agricultural workers answered the Popular Front's slow pace of reform by illegally occupying the estates of traditionalist landowners. In the cities the ranks of the fascist Falange, a party founded in October 1933 that was traditionally more wedded to direct action than conventional political change, swelled and its recruits fought pitched street battles with members of the Communist Party, which had also grown in numbers because of the government's seemingly lukewarm radicalism. Between the election and July around 250 Spaniards were killed in revenge attacks and the sense of chaos increased with the widespread strikes that erupted in May. Neither the politicians of the left or right seemed able to control the worsening situation nor did the influence of extremists of both sides grow, particularly on the right where dissident senior military figures began talking of launching a coup against the Popular Front in March.

The government recognised the danger posed by the military and several likely plot leaders were assigned to posts away from Madrid, the centre of power. Among these were

---

General Francisco Franco (1892–1975)

Franco was a careerist soldier, an officer wedded to reactionary traditions of Catholic, monarchist Spain. He came to prominence during his time with the Spanish Foreign Legion during the Riff Rebellion in Spanish Morocco during the 1920s but his subsequent career up to the outbreak of the civil war reflected the turmoil of Spanish politics. During the right wing dictatorship of General Miguel Primo de Rivera in the late 1920s–early 1930s, he flourished as director of a military academy at Saragossa, but during the time of the left-wing Second Republic he was effectively exiled to the Balearics. Recalled by a new right-wing government elected in late 1933, he played the lead role in suppressing an uprising in the northern Basque region in October the following year and was then made the army's chief-of-staff. The elections of the Popular Front in February 1936 led Franco, who was suspected of planning a coup against the government with his fellow generals, to be sent to the distant Canaries as commander of the islands' garrison. At the outbreak of the civil war in July 1936 the Nationalist rebels in mainland Spain lacked several essential ingredients for success: a clear-cut leader, the experienced professional Army of Africa stuck in Spanish Morocco, and the means to train and equip a large modern fighting force. Franco, the most dynamic of the rebel generals, turned to Nazi Germany and fascist Italy to resolve the latter two weaknesses and in doing so effectively made himself the most obvious choice for leadership of the Nationalist cause. Franco, who still faced right-wing challengers to his authority, was aided in this by Hitler's decision to send training personnel and equipment to him alone. With this patronage, the general formed and headed a united Nationalist government in late September and also became supreme military commander. In mid-November Franco's position was acknowledged by both Germany and Italy, who both recognised the new Nationalist government. The Nationalist victory in 1939 left Franco as Spain's unchallenged ruler and his dictatorship, although increasingly anachronistic in the modern world, survived until his death heralded a new era of Spanish democracy.

Above: Map of Spain showing the major physical features.

General Emilio Mola, who was transferred to the Navarre region in the northeast, General Manuel Goded, who was dispatched to the Balearic Islands, General Luis Orgaz, who was sent to the Canaries as military governor and Franco, who was also transferred to the latter islands as garrison commander. Although the plotters were backed by a larger number of lower-ranking officers who had joined the Spanish Military Union and also enjoyed the tacit support of various leaders of right-wing factions, they lacked an obvious figurehead as the most likely choice, Sanjurjo, was still in exile in Portugal following his leading role in the failed coup of 1932. Equally, success was far from certain as officers loyal to the government had formed the Republican Anti-Fascist Military Union and the authorities had begun moving extra Assault Guards (armed urban police) into Madrid. For the moment, the rebel generals held back from openly declaring against the Popular Front government but as matters deteriorated they continued to prepare for rebellion. Despite the worsening situation on the streets, the government did not act decisively to quell the disorder and in mid-July its inability to control matters was highlighted by the murder of monarchist leader José Calvo Sotelo. Formerly a finance minister in the late 1920s and recently a vocal critic of the Popular Front with links to the military conspiracy, he fell victim to one of the increasingly frequent tit-for-tat killings after Lieutenant José Castillo, an officer in the Assault Guards and member of Anti-Fascist Military Union, was murdered by Falangists on the 12th.

From the 13th, news spread rapidly that Sotelo had been formerly arrested by the Assault Guards and then shot out of hand with no regard to legal procedure. To the right

Above: The main towns and regions of Spain.

wing it confirmed that the government was wholly incapable of exerting control over the state apparatus and the murder hardened the resolve of the plotters to implement their rebellion. The rising, which began a day earlier than planned as the generals feared discovery if they delayed, opened in Spanish Morocco immediately after the completion of manoeuvres by the Army of Africa at Melilla on the 17th. Over the following days both Franco and Orgaz left the Canaries for the North Africa colony. On the 19th a British de Havilland Dragon Rapide passenger plane chartered in Croydon outside London by Luis Bolin, a pro-monarchist journalist, touched down in Tetuán, Spanish Morocco, with Franco on board. He immediately took charge of the Army of Africa as news of the rising spread to the mainland, where similar revolts broke out across the country. On the 23rd a Junkers Ju 52/3m commandeered by the rebels after it touched down at Las Palmas three days earlier also landed at Tetuán. The aircraft, a long-distance passenger carrier of Nazi Germany's Lufthansa civilian airline normally plying the West Africa-Berlin route, was piloted by Flugkapitän Alfred Henke and on board was Orgaz.

Although the situation remained fluid and unclear, the latter part of July saw Spain divided, with roughly 11 million Spaniards out of a total population of 25 million finding themselves in rebel-controlled territory. In the north, the plotters, now widely referred to as Nationalists, gained control of Castile, Navarre and the northwest coast with the important naval base at El Ferrol but failed utterly to secure the Basque northern coast and its interior, which contained various valuable mining and industrial concerns. They also took over western Andalusia in the southwest but this was isolated from the northern

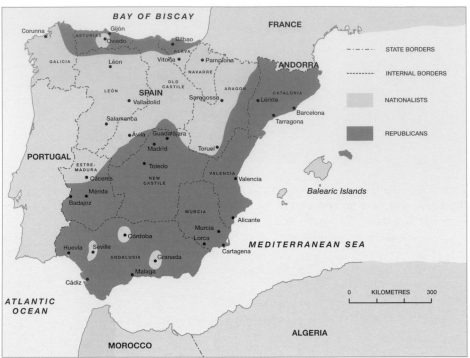

Above: The political position in July 1936: the government controlled the majority of territory, but the Nationalists had the army.

gains by a broad band of Republican territory and, to make matters worse, it was effectively isolated from Spanish Morocco by the Strait of Gibraltar as the Nationalists lacked the means to transfer Franco's Army of Africa to the mainland. Equally, Cadiz, the main port of entry from Spanish Morocco, had been taken by the Nationalists but was surrounded by pro-Republican forces and the only major city secured in western Andalusia was inland Seville. The generals doubted that their coup would meet with sure success under such fractured circumstances and matters were not improved by the death of their supposed head, Sanjurjo, in an air crash on the 20th. Although Mola took charge, his authority was not wholly endorsed by the other generals, leaving a potential power vacuum that might have disastrous consequences for the rebellion.

The generals' coup therefore met with mixed fortunes in its opening phase but militarily, the two sides were fairly evenly matched—at least in terms of ground forces. The regular Spanish Army, which counted territorially based units on the mainland as well as in the Balearics and Canaries, comprised some 60,000 men in 10 divisions. These were split almost evenly between the Republicans and Nationalists but the former could also count on the loyalty of around 50,000 members of Spain's various militarised police forces—the Assault Guards, Civil Guards and Carabineers. The remaining 30,000 police declared for the Nationalists, who could also draw on Franco's 25,000 Army of Africa but for the moment it was stuck in Spanish Morocco for want of either air or sea-going transport. Outside the army, the Nationalists fared less well. The Republic kept control of around two-thirds of the air force's pre-civil war strength, although the types that were available to both sides were generally outdated. The Spanish Navy was also split decisively in favour of the Republicans, who could count on a battleship, three cruisers, 20 destroyers and 12 submarines against a Nationalist strength of one battleship, two cruisers, a single destroyer and a pair of submarines. The former also controlled roughly two-thirds of the country's merchant marine. To the plotters, the balance of non-military strength—in terms of industry, finance and the like—would be with the Republic in the long term and the only saving grace was that the latter was, in the short term at least, unable to bring its advantages to bear due to the chaos that followed the rebellion and the fractious nature of Republican politics. However, the Nationalists were also a loose coalition of conservative and traditionalist factions lacking an overall leader and short of the means to deliver an early knock-out blow before the Republic could marshal its resources. Both sides set about gathering recruits but both were acutely short of the trained officers and modern military equipment that would bring them swift success. The Republic turned to the Soviet Union and France for aid, while the Nationalists looked to Nazi Germany and fascist Italy.

READY FOR WAR

Following the outbreak of the civil war in July 1936, Franco, the most dynamic of the rebel generals, recognised that a Nationalist victory was far from assured and that the most pressing problems were the transfer of the Army of Africa to the Spanish mainland and the need to secure outside military supplies. He turned to two potential suppliers of aircraft, Nazi Germany and fascist Italy, countries whose extreme right-wing leaderships were most likely to look favourably on his request. He made his first efforts to secure German air support on 22 July when one of his subordinates dispatched an urgent message to the German military attaché in Paris requesting '10 transports with maximum seating capacity'. The Nationalists suggested that they might buy them through private German firms but that the aircraft would have to be flown to Spanish Morocco by German pilots. Franco also decided to make a direct plea to Hitler. Fortuitously, Henke and his Ju 52/3m were still at Tetuán and on 23 July three men left in this civilian passenger aircraft with Henke again at the controls to seek a personal audience with Adolf Hitler and present him with a letter from Franco. These emissaries comprised Captain Francisco Arranz, a Nationalist air force officer, Adolph Langenheim, leader of the Nazi Party in Tetuán, and Johannes Bernhardt, now head of the Nazi Party's foreign department in Morocco but previously a disgraced former sugar merchant from Hamburg who had turned to making a living by selling kitchen stoves to the local garrison in Spanish Morocco. Franco proved wise to contact Hitler directly as it soon became apparent that the German foreign ministry was reluctant to become embroiled in the looming Spanish conflict as it might spark the outbreak of war across Europe. The

Below: *Deutschland* leaves for Spain through the Kaiser Wilhelm canal. *via Jak Mallmann-Showell*

acting head of the German war ministry went so far as to inform his counterpart in the foreign ministry that sending aid to the Nationalists was 'out of the question'. Franco's three emissaries to Hitler were delayed in Seville after their aircraft developed engine trouble but finally arrived in Berlin late on the 24th. Following diplomatic protocol, Franco's letter was passed to the war ministry and, once again, its head made his objections abundantly plain, as did the foreign minister, Constantin Freiherr von Neurath. However, other Nazi officials were of a different view. Franco's team met Rudolf Hess, Hitler's deputy and he arranged for the delegation to have an audience with the Führer. The ultimate decision to support the Nationalists undoubtedly lay

Auslaufen durch Kaiser-Wilhelm-Kanal

Above: *Graf Spee* seen in May 1937. Launched in 1934 she was the third and last of the German 'pocket battleships'. Armed with 6 x 28cm and 8 x 15cm guns she also carried two Arado Ar 196s. While raiding shipping off the coast of Uruguay on 13 December 1939 she was caught by the Royal Navy ships HMSs *Exeter*, *Ajax* and *Achilles* in the Battle of the River Plate. Taking damage she sought shelter and repairs in Montevideo harbour, but forced to leave and rather than have her captured her Captain Hans Langsdorff scuttled her on 17 December.

Life

Laid down: Reichsmarinewerft Wilhelmshaven, 01.10.1932
Launched: 30.06.1934
Commissioned: 06.01.1936
Fate: scuttled 17.12.1939 (La Plate estuary)
Costs: RM 82 million

Commanders

KptzS Konrad Patzig: Jan 1936–Oct 1937
KptzS Walter Warzecha: Oct 1937–Oct 1938
KptzS Hans Langsdorf: Oct 1938–17.12.1939

with the German leader, who finally met Franco's party late on the 25th after attending a performance of Richard Wagner's opera *Siegfried* in Bayreuth. Hermann Göring, chief of the fledgling Luftwaffe, was also present. He was keen to test his young command in battle but was wary of embroilment as it might overstretch his forces. The decision to aid Franco was taken that night, although most of those present were acutely aware that German involvement, even though envisaged as being covert, brief and on a limited scale, might provoke a Europe-wide crisis and even a general war.

Over the subsequent years Hitler gave several reasons to explain his motives: to divert the attention of the major European powers away from his rearmament programme; to prevent the spread of Communism in Europe; to aid the creation of a friendly state that would threaten the security of sea routes linking Britain and France with their colonies in Africa and beyond; and to secure supplies of Spanish iron ore for Germany's military expansion. There may also have been a degree of egotism in the decision. Certainly, the cap-in-hand plea from Franco played to Hitler's vanity at a time when he was being mostly cold-shouldered on the wider European scene, not least because of the Nazi reoccupation of the demilitarised Rhineland in early March.

After the Bayreuth meeting, matters progressed swiftly. The scale and organisation of the covert operation was left to the *Reichsluftfahrtministerium* (RLM/Reich Air Travel Ministry), where General der Flieger Erhard Milch held the first discussions on the matter during the evening of the 26th. Those present concluded that the Nationalists needed at least 20 Ju 52s flown by Lufthansa pilots and supported by various ground personnel to effect the transfer of the Army of Africa from Spanish Morocco. Generalleutnant Helmut Wilberg, code-named Wilde, was empowered to organise a bureau known as *Sonderstab W* (Special Staff Wilberg) to deal with the practicalities of sourcing both the aircraft and personnel to undertake the mission, which became known as Operation '*Feuerzauber*' (Magic Fire). For supply shipments, two companies were established. HISMA (*Companía Hispano-Marroquí de Transportes*/Spanish-Moroccan Transport Company), a joint German-Spanish venture, was set up in late July to oversee the delivery of the aircraft and associated equipment, market them in Spain and collect payments, either money or raw materials, from the Nationalists. It was initially based at Tetuán before moving to Seville. Bernhardt, who had always hoped to gain financially from his role as an emissary to Hitler, travelled to mainland Spain as HISMA's general manager. A second but wholly German body, ROWAK (*Rohstoffe-und-Waren-Einkaufsgesellschaft*/Raw Materials and Goods Purchasing Company), was established in early October and given responsibility for buying supplies for Spain in Germany. So secret were their initial operations that neither the German foreign ministry nor the economic ministry became aware of their activities until some time late in October; only the finance ministry knew of their efforts as it had credited ROWAK with three million Reichsmarks to begin its buying mission.

THE FIRST GERMAN VOLUNTEERS

The recruitment and dispatch of volunteers was undertaken in equal secrecy by a body known as the *Reisegesellschaftsunion* (Tourist Party Union) and Oberst Alexander von Scheele, who later became military head of HISMA, was ordered to take charge of the first contingent to head for Spain. As early as 27 July a call for pilots was sent out to fighter units based at Dortmund and Berlin-Döberitz and bomber squadrons at Neukirchen-bei-Ansbach, Gotha and Merseburg. Two days later the first Luftwaffe volunteers, just 86 men (10 bomber crews led by Oberleutnant Rudolf Freiherr von Moreau, six fighter pilots and various non-flying support personnel) assembled at Döberitz and on the 31st, dressed in civilian clothes and with no idea of their destination, they boarded the passenger vessel *Usaramo* at Hamburg. Apart from the volunteers, the steamship carried six Heinkel He 51

Above: Generalmajor Hugo Sperrle photographed during an early visit to the Luftwaffe volunteers in Spain. Sperrle had been appointed by Göring to command the Legion and although Luftwaffe Oberst von Scheele had commanded the first detachment of German volunteers to serve in Spain, Sperrle took command from November 1936. *via Brian L. Davies*

biplane fighters, 20 Flak 30 2 cm light anti-aircraft guns and around 100 tons of other supplies when it sailed on 1 August. Nearing southern Spain four days later, the *Usaramo* was escorted on the final leg of its journey by the Kriegsmarine's *Deutschland* and the torpedo-boats *Leopard* and *Luchs* and, after docking in the harbour of Nationalist-controlled Cadiz on the 6th, the men and equipment headed north to Seville by train. The city had recently fallen to the Nationalists and the Germans set up camp at nearby Tablada airfield, where 10 Ju 52 transport had recently arrived from Germany by way of San Remo in Italy to begin the airlift of Franco's troops from Tetuán.

From September, Germany's commitment to the Nationalist cause grew steadily and drew in men and equipment from the Wehrmacht's other branches and 'Feuerzauber' was renamed Operation 'Guido' from early November. A similar pattern of secret recruitment

Below: One of the Kriegsmarine's torpedo boats moored in Cadiz harbour. *via Jak Mallmann-Showell*

Above: Formation of He 60 floatplanes over a German submarine. The He 60s stated to arrive during October 1936 to protect shipping heading for mainland Spain. *TRH Pictures*

was followed in the army, with most of the initial batch of volunteers being drawn from 4th and 6th Panzer Regiments. The raising of these men had initially devolved on Oberst Walther Warlimont, who was codenamed 'Guido', but in late September he moved to become Germany's chief representative on Franco's staff and was replaced by Wilhelm Josef Ritter von Thoma, a World War 1 veteran who had recently served with various units of Germany's emerging tank force. None of those answering the call was told of either his destination or role and, as with the Luftwaffe recruits, it was not envisaged that the volunteers would undertake combat roles but rather were to train the Spanish Nationalists in the techniques of modern warfare and how to operate German equipment. Dressed in civilian clothes, the men assembled in Berlin, where they were provided with 200 Reichsmarks for expenses, given passports and then split into small groups for the next stage of their journey to Stettin, northeast of the capital, by bus. On 2 September the first army recruits, now divided into the 1st and 2nd Panzer Companies, boarded the steamships *Girgenti* and *Passages* for the voyage to Spain. The vessels carried around 180 volunteers plus a consignment of 41 Panzer PzKpfw IA and IB light tanks, transport, workshop equipment and 20 light anti-tank guns. Later joined by a further tank company, radio detachments and large numbers of anti-tank guns, the army contingent was split into two main groups. *Gruppe Imker* (Group Beekeeper) was the cover designation given to the various training units sent to the Nationalists, while von Thoma's tank-training companies were known as *Gruppe Drohne* (Group Drone).

As with the Luftwaffe and the army, the Spanish Nationalists also received vital aid from the Kriegsmarine as much of Spain's pre-civil war navy had remained loyal to the

Republican cause. The initial approach was made by the pro-Franco naval attaché in Paris, Lieutenant Commander Arturo Génova, who had resigned his post on 17 July and returned to Spain in early August to fight for the Nationalist cause. He was on close terms with Admiral Wilhelm Canaris, the head of German military intelligence, and the two had discussed Germany loaning the Nationalists two submarines. Despite Canaris's best efforts, Génova's request for German naval aid was initially rebuffed by the chief of the *Oberkommando der Kriegsmarine* (OKM/Navy High Command), Konteradmiral Günther Grusse. He was initially wary of overt aid to the Nationalists for fear of sparking a full-blown international crisis but matters changed on 24 October when the Italian foreign minister, Count Ciano, met Hitler to sign the Rome-Berlin Axis and informed the German leader that Italy was sending sizeable forces, including submarines, to support the Nationalists. The Kriegsmarine was ordered to Spain and this aid, which began to flow from November, took several forms. Firstly, in an operation codenamed '*Nordsee*' (North Sea), numerous instructors travelled to Spain to teach Franco's naval personnel the arts of naval and coastal gunnery, mine warfare and the deployment of torpedo-boats. Secondly, the Kriegsmarine took over the responsibility for co-ordinating the movement of German army and air force personnel and equipment to Spain, either directly to Nationalist-held ports or by way of neighbouring Portugal. Thirdly, the Kriegsmarine provided various surface ships to protect convoys ferrying Franco's Army of Africa from Spanish Morocco to the mainland and a range of warships took part in these missions, including the *Admiral Scheer* and *Deutschland*, both of which carried members of the North Sea group. Finally, and most secretively of all, German U-boats were dispatched to Spanish waters in an operation codenamed '*Ursula*' after the daughter of Karl Dönitz, founding father of Nazi Germany's submarine force.

Selected German supply ships to Spain, August-November 1936 (1)

Vessel	Destination	Arrival	Cargo
Usaramo	Cadiz	August 6	86 personnel; 6 x Heinkel He 51 fighters; 20 x 2 cm anti-aircraft guns; 100 tons of various other supplies.
Girgenti (2)	Corunna	August 26	Eight million rounds of ammunition; 10,000 rifles; 10,000 stick grenades.
Kamerun	Lisbon (3)	August 30	Aviation fuel.
Wigbert	Lisbon	August 30	2 x Junkers Ju 52 transport/bombers; 15 external bomb racks; 372 tons of aviation fuel; radio equipment.
Usaramo	Cadiz	early September	20 x Heinkel He 46 biplane reconnaissance aircraft for the Nationalists; various aviation spares; ammunition; radio equipment; chemicals.
Passages/Girgenti	Cadiz	late September	180 personnel; 41 x Panzer PzKpfw I light tanks; 20 x 2 cm anti-tank guns; vehicles; workshop equipment.
Fulda (4)	Cadiz	mid-November	100 vehicles and various personnel.

1) Most of the initial supplies were shipped from Hamburg but other ports were used subsequently, including Stettin and Swinemünde.
2) Many of these supplies were provided by a private entrepreneur, Josef Veltjens, but Franco was quickly persuaded by Generalleutnant Helmut Wilberg to accept shipment from only official Nazi channels.
3) Following diplomatic pressure from the British, the Portuguese dictator Antonio de Oliveira Salazar closed Lisbon to German supplies destined for the Nationalists at the end of August.
4) This was the 21st German supply ship sent to Spain but the first to carry members of the newly constituted Condor Legion. A further 25 vessels with extra personnel, weapons, munitions and other supplies reached the peninsula by the end of the month. Vigo on the northwest coast became the major point of entry for German supplies along with Cadiz.

IN ACTION

What followed Hitler's decision to help Franco in late July 1936 was the first major airlift of troops and equipment in military history, one that had a significant early impact on the civil war and undoubtedly aided the Nationalist cause in general and Franco in particular. On the 27th Henke took off from Berlin at the controls of his Ju 52 and headed back to Spanish Morocco to support the small but ongoing movement of Nationalist troops to the mainland being undertaken by a motley collection of a few antiquated aircraft and commandeered vessels. The next day the lone Ju 52, which had been stripped of all interior fittings to accommodate 35 men sitting on the floor of its cramped interior, transferred the first batch of Nationalist troops from their base at Tetuán to the mainland. Henke's transport was soon joined by a second and over the next 14 days the pair moved some 2,489 troops of the Army of Africa. During the following weeks more Ju 52s followed in Henke's footsteps by flying from Germany to either Spain or Spanish Morocco by way of refuelling stops in San Remo, Italy, and the lift gathered momentum. By the close of August around 20 German transports were in operation, all flying under the immediate control of Hauptmann Rudolf Freiherr von Moreau. He had arrived at Cadiz on the 6th aboard the SS *Usaramo*, which had left Hamburg on the last day of July with

Below: A rifle section of the Army of Africa boards a Ju 52. *via Austin Brown Photo Library*

half a dozen Heinkel He 51B fighters, six further Ju 52s, and a score of Flak 30 2 cm anti-aircraft guns as its chief cargo. The fighters were taken from several Luftwaffe units, chiefly *Jagdgeschwader* (JG/Fighter Group) 132 'Richthofen' and JG 134 'Horst Wessel', while the Ju 52s were sourced from *Kampfgeschwader* (KG/Bomber Group) 153, KG 155 and KG 253 'General Wever'. In addition, the ship carried 25 Luftwaffe officers and 66 non-commissioned officers, other ranks and civilian experts under Oberst Alexander von Scheele who were to instruct their Spanish counterparts in all aspects of aerial warfare. Moreau immediately travelled to Seville, where Franco had established his own command post, and from where several flights to North Africa were co-ordinated each day. He immediately set about making maximum use of his small command. Moreau himself travelled to Tetuán to take charge of the Ju 52 transport. Henke was ordered to begin training Spanish pilots to use 10 Ju 52s as bombers, Oberleutnant Kraft Eberhardt was sent to Tablada airfield outside Seville to establish training facilities for Nationalist fighter pilots and oversee communications and supply systems, while Leutnant Hans-Joachim Herrmann was ordered to train the Spanish in the use of the anti-aircraft guns at the same base.

The Luftwaffe officers' brief soon expanded to cover much more than the transports of men and equipment from Spanish Morocco to the mainland and train the Nationalists in all aspects of aerial warfare. As the Republicans controlled much of the pre-civil war navy and the strength of their air power was not precisely known, Moreau took action to ensure the continuation of the ferry system. Aided by Italian bombers, he organised top-cover patrols to protect the Nationalist transports from enemy aircraft and warships and also fitted out a pair of Ju 52s, which could also act as bombers, for a strike at a potentially dangerous Republican warship. Shortly after 0400 hours on 13 August two Ju 52s flown by Henke and Moreau and each carrying six 550 lb (250 kg) bombs on improvised external racks set out from Tablada for Republican-controlled Malaga, the base of *Jaime I*, the only major enemy warship close to the Strait of Gibraltar. Moreau failed to reach the target area but at around dawn Henke scored two hits on the warship from 1,500 ft (500 m), damaging its upper deck and killing 47 of its crew. *Jaime I* was moved northeastward to Cartagena for repair, a far greater distance from the Strait of Gibraltar than Malaga. After this decisive intervention, other Republic warships proved reluctant to interfere with the sea transports partly because of the command chaos that followed their crews' successful mutinies against their mostly Nationalist officers and also the threatening presence of German warships in the area of potential operations.

The airlift of Franco's forces from Tetuán by Moreau escalated rapidly following the Luftwaffe's intervention, although the effort was bedevilled by fuel shortages and poor facilities that made maintenance extremely difficult. An early stopgap was provided by fuel garnered from neighbouring French Morocco but this proved inadequate and Moreau's transports were grounded for two days, although matters improved somewhat from mid-August after aviation fuel and oil from Germany and Italy had arrived in Spanish Morocco by tanker. Despite these ongoing problems, a routine was soon established. The Ju 52s were mostly active in the mornings and evenings as their heavy loads put them at risk from the high winds that often blew during the heat of the day.

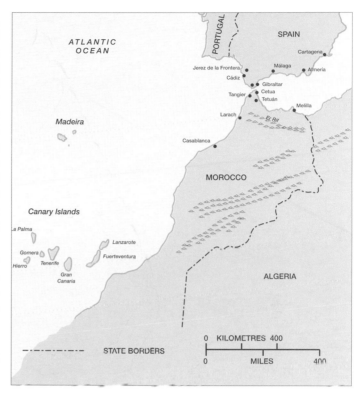

Above: The Luftwaffe's involvement in the airlift of the Army of Africa from Morocco to mainland Spain was critical to the success of the operation.

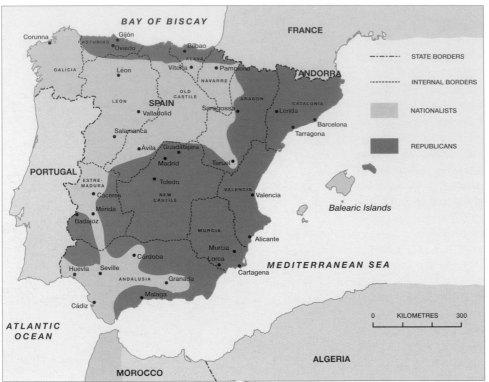

Above: The arrival of the Army of Africa had an immediate effect on the political map of southern Spain; the position is shown in August-September 1936. See also the map on page 20 showing the march of the army to Madrid.

Consequently, aircrews crammed their flights to the mainland into these two periods and their only breaks occurred during loading or taking on more fuel. Essential maintenance was conducted at night under the inadequate glare of lanterns or headlights. For the first five days of operations the transports flew from Tetuán to Seville in 60 minutes or so at heights of between 8,000 ft and 11,500 ft (2,500–3,500 m) to avoid enemy fire and covering a distance of some 110 miles (176 km), but the establishment of an airstrip at Jerez de la Frontera south of Seville reduced the distance by 30 miles (48 km) and the flight time dropped by 20 minutes. The transfer of Franco's troops hit an early high in the week 10–16 August, when some 400 men flew out from Tetuán each day, but thereafter, it averaged between 1,200 and 1,600 every seven days. Priorities changed at the end of the month and for much of September Moreau's crews concentrated on flying in supplies, an effort that reached its peak between the 14th and 20th when some 70 tons reached the mainland. The flights continued for several more weeks, officially ending on 11 October, by which time some 13,500 Nationalist troops, 127 machine guns, 36 field guns and tons of other vital stores had been carried across the strait. The Ju 52s had flown 868 sorties in total and losses had been remarkably light, just the one aircraft that had crashed after stalling during take-off at Jerez de la Frontera on 15 August killing two corporals, Helmut Schulze and Herbert Zech. Hitler later suggested that Franco should erect a monument to the Ju 52 for its part in saving the Nationalist cause.

GERMANY'S GROWING COMMITMENT

AAlthough the Luftwaffe expeditionary forces had been under strict orders to avoid combat operations, the period of the airlift also saw them undertake direct action against the Republicans chiefly because of the limited air expertise of the Nationalists. The attack on *Jaime I* was one example but there were others: on 20 and 21 August Moreau flew a Ju 52 laden with rations to Toledo, where a small Nationalist garrison was holding out in the city's Alcazar fortress, and on the night of the 27th/28th he flew to Madrid to bomb the Republican Air Ministry. The Luftwaffe's volunteer fighter pilots were also exceeding their non-combatant brief. At Tablada, it quickly became apparent to Eberhardt that his Spanish pupils were far from proficient pilots. A number of the He 51s had been written off because of their inexperience including a pair on 22 August, and, rather than risk further losses, Eberhardt and two of his colleagues, Trautloft and Leutnant Herwig Knüppel, took direct action. Two days later they escorted eight Spanish-crewed Ju 52s on a bombing raid against Getafe airfield south of Madrid; the following day Eberhardt and Trautloft each shot down a Republican aircraft. By the 27th the Luftwaffe pilots had claimed four more kills, although the slide from support to combat roles flew in the face of the previously agreed German policy. Nevertheless, on the 29th, Hitler officially backed the use of Luftwaffe crews on combat operations and at the end of the month Scheele, who had been unable to prevent the gradual slide into offensive action and seemed out of his depth in Spain, was replaced by a new officer, Oberstleutnant Walter Warlimont. His orders were to head Operation '*Guido*', a body that was given both military and diplomatic responsibilities at the heart of Franco's headquarters.

Above: Ju 52s flying towards Spain. When the airlift stopped on 11 October over 17,000 troops had been transported—and saved the Nationalists' from extinction. The aircraft in the background is 22 • 59. *via Austin Brown Photo Library*

German military aid also increased during August, most notably after General der Flieger Helmuth Wilberg paid a visit to Franco. In the middle of the month more than 155 tons of bombs and bomb racks were unloaded at Lisbon, and with the tacit co-operation of the country's right-wing dictator Antonio de Oliveira Salazar, transported into Nationalist-controlled Spain. In September a further 86 tons of bombs arrived, together with searchlights and a battery of 8.8 cm anti-aircraft guns under Hauptmann Aldinger. Equally noteworthy was the arrival of Oberstleutnant Ritter von Thoma on the 20th. He was charged with training Nationalist forces in various aspects of modern ground warfare, particularly the use of armour, and by the end of the month more than 40 Panzer PzKpfw I tanks, an anti-tank unit and 122 personnel had also been disembarked. More aircraft also arrived during this period, rising from 36 during July and August, to 44 in September and 28 in October. Some of these were passed to the Nationalists but the German volunteers also received more aircraft and formed new combat units. In September Moreau took charge of a *Kette* (flight) of three Ju 52 and this small force formed the basis of what was christened *Gruppe Moreau* and later consisted of 20 of the bombers and a pair of Heinkel He 70F reconnaissance/bomber aircraft. German fighter strength also rose and by the end of the month 14 He 51s formed what was known as *Gruppe Eberhardt*. During October Heinkel He 60 floatplanes began arriving to protect German shipping heading for mainland Spain.

THE STRUGGLE FOR MADRID

Meanwhile, after arriving in Seville in early August Franco ordered an advance on Madrid by around 8,000 troops, mostly men from the Army of Africa under General Juan Yagüe. Five lorry-borne columns backed by 75 mm artillery were ordered to move northward from Seville at utmost speed by way of Mérida, some 200 miles (320 km) from Franco's headquarters, and then strike northeastward towards the capital, which was still largely undefended. Yagüe's troops were supported by Ju 52s flown by German crews and made astonishing progress; village after village held by Republican militia were simply overrun in quick time by his ruthless professionals. By the 10th the Nationalists had reached the outskirts of Mérida and, after diverting to capture Badajoz from the Republicans, brushed aside the defenders of Mérida and reached the Tagus valley by the 23rd. Yagüe now

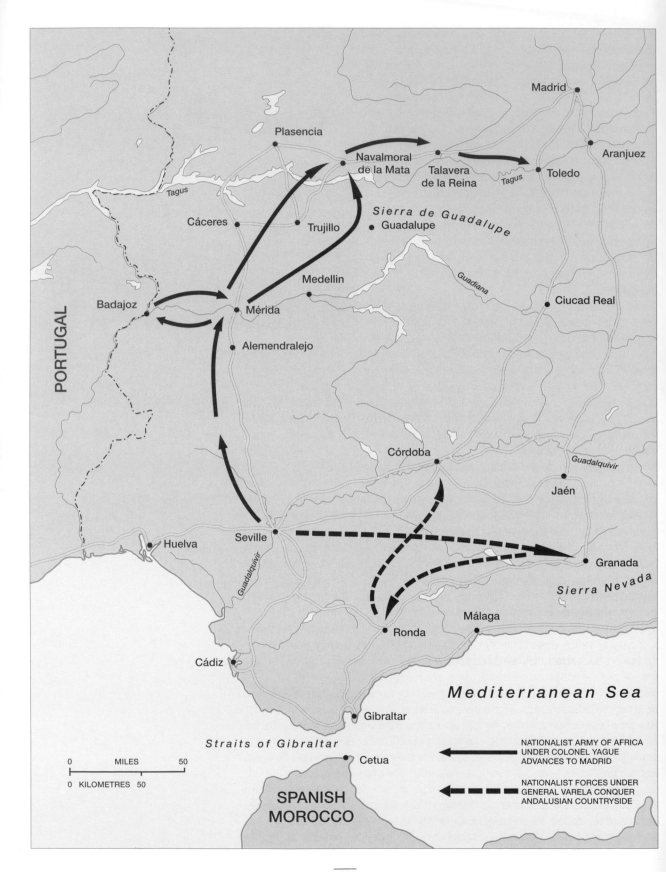

PORTUGAL

Plasencia

Madrid

Navalmoral
de la Mata

Talavera
de la Reina

Aranjuez

Toledo

Tagus

Tagus

Cáceres

Trujillo

Guadalupe

Sierra de Guadalupe

Medellin

Guadiana

Ciucad Real

Badajoz

Mérida

Alemendralejo

Córdoba

Guadalquivir

Jaén

Seville

Huelva

Granada

Guadalquivir

Sierra Nevada

Ronda

Málaga

Cádiz

Mediterranean Sea

Gibraltar

Straits of Gibraltar

Cetua

NATIONALIST ARMY OF AFRICA
UNDER COLONEL YAGUE
ADVANCES TO MADRID

NATIONALIST FORCES UNDER
GENERAL VARELA CONQUER
ANDALUSIAN COUNTRYSIDE

0   MILES   50

0   KILOMETRES   50

SPANISH
MOROCCO

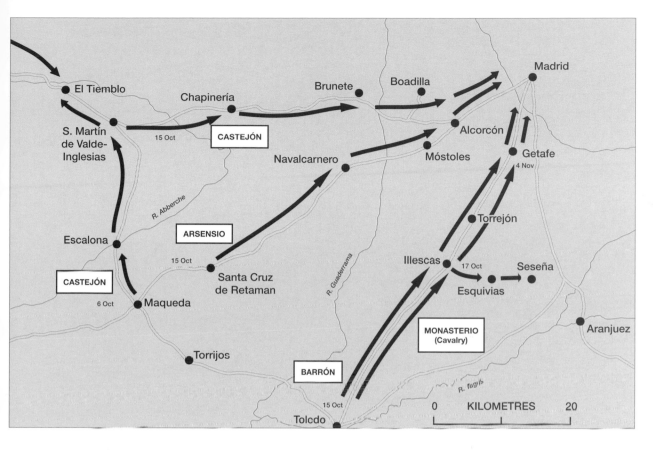

swung northeastward along the valley and captured Talavera de la Reina, the last town of any significance before Madrid, on September 3. The capital, just 60 miles (96 km) distant, was largely undefended but Franco ordered Yagüe to switch his axis of attack towards Toledo to relieve the defenders of the Alcazar. Air support was once again provided by German-crewed Ju 52s and the siege of the Alcazar was finally broken on 28 September. After this controversial but successful diversion to relieve the Alcazar, Franco resumed his push towards what was by now a much more strongly defended Madrid. On 2 November, Brunete to the west of the capital fell to the Nationalists and two days later the airfield at Getafe to the south was captured. The Nationalist troops established positions to the immediate west of the city's centre and on the 8th they attacked in strength on a narrow front. Three main columns, some 26,000 men supported by Italian-crewed tankettes and some of von Thoma's recently arrived Panzer PzKpfw Is, struck across the Casa de Campo to take the University area and the Plaza de Espana and, although outnumbered some two-to-one, the Nationalists expected to quickly rout the motley collection of ill-armed Republican forces opposing them. However, the defenders proved more resolute than expected and the Nationalists made little progress. Over the following days, Franco's forces redoubled their efforts to take the capital but the Republicans, who were bolstered by the arrival of the first volunteer units of the International Brigades, stood firm. Faced by mounting losses and little progress, Franco called off the battle on the 19th.

The faltering Nationalist ground attack on Madrid in November had been matched by a sudden decisive swing in favour of the Republican air force. In October two Soviet freighters had docked in Bilbao and Cartagena and disgorged their cargoes and passengers, some 55 Polikarpov I-15 fighters and the experienced Russian pilots to fly

Above: The Nationalists advance on Madrid, October-November 1936.

Opposite left: The path of the Army of Africa, August-September 1936.

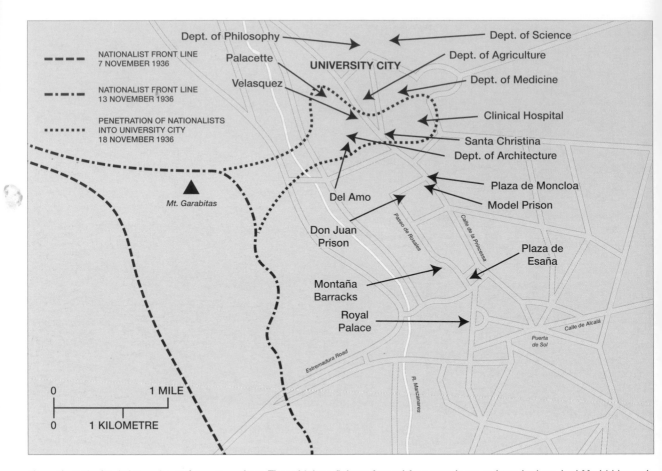

Above: The Battle of Madrid, November 1936. In spite of great efforts, Madrid stayed Republican. Had the Army of Africa marched directly to the capital and attacked, then the story — if not the outcome — of the civil war could have been very different.

them. These biplane fighters formed four squadrons and two had reached Madrid by early November. On their first sortie on the 4th they shot down three Nationalist aircraft, one of which was a German Ju 52 piloted by Leutnant Oskar Kolbitz. As further Soviet aircraft and pilots made their way to the capital, two more Ju 52s were downed on the 8th. Although not of the most modern design, these Polikarpovs generally outmatched the Nationalist opposition and began to score an increasing number of victories. Among the German casualties were Eberhardt and Oskar Henrici. Both men had themselves notched up several kills—seven and four respectively—but their Heinkel He 51s were beaten in a dogfight with I-15s on 13 November. Eberhardt collided with one enemy fighter he had shot down and failed to bail out before crashing while Henrici was shot through a lung and, although able to land in friendly territory, died shortly after exiting his aircraft. To add to the Nationalists' woes, a second batch of fighters comprising 31 Polikarpov I-16 Type 5 monoplanes, sufficient to form a further three squadrons, entered combat on the 16th.

The situation around Madrid in late 1936 greatly affected Germany's commitment to Franco and the Nationalist cause. What had hitherto been a relatively ad hoc package of military aid was transformed into a major and much more organised effort even as the battle for the capital intensified. The expansion of the German mission had begun in September when Warlimont travelled to Berlin and argued for more men and equipment to offset the flow of supplies being sent to the Republicans by the Soviet Union. Several senior Nazis, especially Göring, opposed such a move, and Warlimont returned to Spain seemingly without securing any agreement. Matters changed following Hitler's formal recognition of the Nationalist government that Franco established on the 30th. Desperate for Nazi aid to support his war effort, Franco agreed to the creation of an independent

German force. The 'Feuerzauber' and 'Guido' commands were subsumed into a new organisation known as Winterübung Rügen (Winter Exercise Rügen) and those units already in Spain were taken over by a new combat force that was briefly codenamed Eiserne Rationen (Iron Rations). This was then renamed Eiserne Legion (Iron Legion) but Göring intervened and chose a new title—Condor Legion. In early November some 4,500 more Luftwaffe volunteers arrived in Spain as well as 20 Ju 52s, 14 He 51s, six He 45 reconnaissance aircraft and two floatplanes, an He 59 and an He 60. Further reinforcements arrived over the following weeks and the organisation of the German force was regularised. The Condor Legion comprised Kampfgruppe 88 (K/88) with three Staffeln (squadrons) of Ju 52 bombers, Jagdgruppe 88 (J/88) with three squadrons of He 51s fighters, Aufklärungsgruppe 88 (A/88/Reconnaissance Group 88) with two reconnaissance squadrons, one of fast Heinkel He 70 monoplanes and the other of slower Heinkel He 45 biplanes, and Aufklärungsstaffel See 88 (AS/88) comprising a handful of reconnaissance floatplanes. Further support was provided by an anti-aircraft group, Flakabteilung 88 (F/88) consisting of four batteries of 8.8 cm guns and two of 2 cm light cannon, a signals detachment—Nachrichtenabteilung 88 (Ln/88) and various support groups. The He 51s and Ju 52s already in Spain were incorporated into this new structure, forming the four Staffeln of J/88 and K/88 respectively. Overall command of the Legion rested with Generalmajor Hugo Sperrle, whose chief of staff was named as Oberstleutnant Alexander Holle. Sperrle's arrival in Seville on 5 November also signalled the departure of Henke, who returned to German and resumed service as a Lufthansa pilot, and the transfer of Scheele, who was named as the German air attaché and was based in Salamanca.

Top Left and Right: The Spanish Civil War is known for the graphic art both sides produced in posters. That above left was issued by the Comite Nacional; above right by the Delyoda de Defensa. TRH Pictures

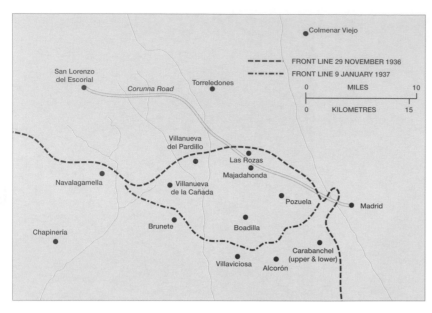

Colmenar Viejo

- - - - - FRONT LINE 29 NOVEMBER 1936
-·-·-·- FRONT LINE 9 JANUARY 1937

San Lorenzo
del Escorial

Corunna Road

Torreledones

0   MILES   10

0   KILOMETRES   15

Villanueva
del Pardillo

Las Rozas

Majadahonda

Navalagamella

Villanueva
de la Cañada

Pozuela

Madrid

Chapinería

Brunete

Boadilla

Carabanchel
(upper & lower)

Villaviciosa

Alcorón

Above: The Battle of Corunna Road showing the advances made over the Christmas 1936/37 period.

Yet for all these ongoing developments, the situation around Madrid in November caused considerable concern to the Nationalists. Their ground offensive had clearly stalled and in frustration Franco ordered bombing raids on the capital by Italian aircraft and the Ju 52s of the Legion's K/88 to force a collapse in Republican morale. From the 19th until the 23rd the capital was repeatedly hit from the air in what was the first sustained and intense bombing of a city. Hundreds of buildings were destroyed and many people killed yet this aerial barrage singularly failed to produce the wholesale panic or a collapse in morale among either the Republican defenders or the ordinary civilians that Franco desired and he decided to force the issue by launching another ground offensive. At the end of the month the Nationalists struck to the northwest of Madrid with the intention of severing the road running between the capital and Corunna. The first attack was launched on the 29th when 3,000 Army of Africa troops struck towards the village of Pozuelo but, despite support from tanks, artillery and Legion Ju 52 bombers that led to wholesale withdrawals by the front-line defenders, the initial gains were lost when the Republicans launched a counter-attack spearheaded by Soviet T-26 tanks. Nor could the fact be ignored that the Soviet I-15s and I-16s were clearly gaining command of the skies. Before their arrival, the German pilots flying He 51s had notched up a good number of kills. Knüppel had a tally of five, while Henrici, von Houwald and Trautloft had each scored four victories but the arrival of the Soviet fighters brought a sudden end to such successes and claimed several German lives. The inescapable truth was that several Luftwaffe aircraft were not up to the task in hand, most notably the He 45 and He 51 biplanes and the Ju 52 in its day bomber role. Even the 18 He 70s of A/88 were proving troublesome. Although a fast monoplane design, they were comparatively untested and proved mechanically unreliable.

It was perhaps fortunate that these difficulties coincided with the debut of several newer designs. Many were undergoing testing in Germany but the Luftwaffe high command saw the civil war as an ideal opportunity to assess their capabilities under true combat conditions. From late 1936 until the spring of the following year the first of these new aircraft arrived in Spain. In December five Henschel Hs 123 dive-bombers arrived in Seville and were subsequently attached to K/88. Rather than operating in their chosen role, they were flown on ground-attack strafing duties with considerable success. Later the same month a single pre-production prototype of the Heinkel He 112 appeared and, more significantly, three pre-production Messerschmitt Bf 109s were delivered. No further He 112s were sent but the single example, which was attached to J/88's 2nd Staffel, did score some successes. On 28 April 1937, for example its pilot at the time, Oberleutnant Günther Radusch, claimed victory over a I-15. However, the He 112 was already being overshadowed by the Bf 109s. After the three prototypes had proved more than acceptable they returned to Germany in February 1937, but the first of a 45-strong batch of Bf 109Bs arrived in Seville during March. These first arrivals were attached to J/88's 2 Staffel and its commander, Oberleutnant Günther Lützow, claimed the first of their many victories on April 14 after shooting down one of the feared I-15s. The Legion's bomber force was also modernised during this period. First to arrive in February were 30 Heinkel He 111B twin-engined medium bombers, which were used to replace two Ju 52 Staffeln in K/88 and made their combat debut on 9 March by attacking Nationalist airfields at Alcala and Barajos. The He 111s were matched by 15 Dornier Do 17F reconnaissance/bomber types, which were used to replace the 12 He 70s that equipped one of A/88's Staffeln. The final batch to arrive during this period was a score of Dornier Do 17E bombers and these were deployed with 1. and 2. Staffeln of K/88. The replacement of old for new aircraft established a pattern that was followed for the remainder of the war––as the Luftwaffe's modern types arrived their redundant predecessors were passed on to

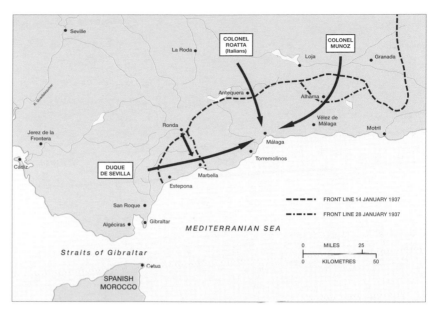

Franco's air force. Thus, for example, the 12 He 70s passed to Nationalist pilots who were sent to support the offensive against Republican-held Malaga.

Above: The Malaga campaign, January–February 1937.

JARAMA AND GUADALAJARA

While the Condor Legion was re-equipping in early 1937, the Nationalists opened a new battlefront along the Jarama valley to the south of the capital. General José Varela was ordered to strike from west to east towards the Jarama river, cross it and sever the road linking Madrid to Valencia. The offensive opened on 6 February and Varela thrust some 25,000 men into the five-pronged attack. Additional ground support came from two batteries of German heavy machine guns, von Thoma's tank force and the Legion's Flak 36 8.8 cm anti-aircraft guns, which were making their combat debut in support of a ground offensive, and the Legion's aircraft were also deployed. The initial attacks made excellent progress, especially on the flanks, in part thanks to K/88's Ju 52s being used to strike Republican units moving up to the battlefront during daylight. The west bank of the Jarama was reached by the morning of the 8th but the momentum was then lost for 48 hours due to heavy rains that made the river unfordable. On the 11th the three Nationalist columns in the centre resumed their attacks and two captured bridges over the Jarama at Pindoque and near San Martin de la Vega. Republican fighters repeatedly strafed follow-on Nationalist troops as they crossed the bridges but suffered considerable losses to the Legion's 8.8 cm flak guns. Once across the river at San Martin, the Nationalists seized the high ground of Pingarron but the thrust over the Pindoque bridge was halted by the Republican International Brigades on the slopes of the Pajares Heights. Despite suffering significant casualties, the Nationalists struggled to break through Republican lines throughout the 12th and 13th but the only success occurred around the southern edge of the Pajares where the assault was aided by 155 mm artillery and a Legion machine gun battery placed on La Maranosa, a piece of high ground to the west of the Jarama. Yet this success was isolated and short-lived. On the 14th the Republicans flung 50 Soviet-supplied T-26s at the breach in their line with the intention of regaining the bridge at Pindoque, thereby stalling the Nationalist advance and allowing further Republican forces to be fed into the battle. The tanks did not reach Pindoque in part due

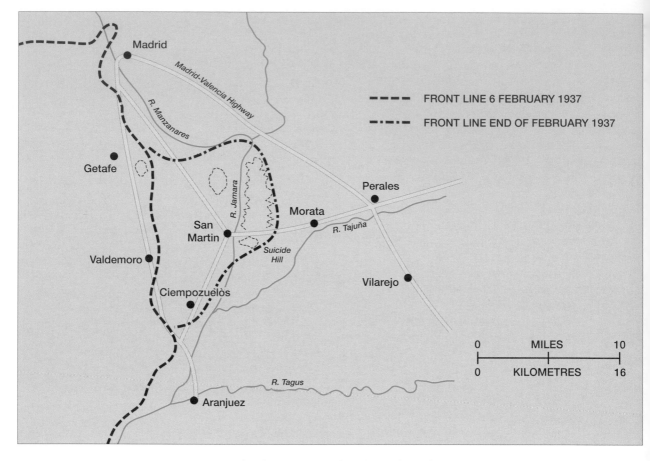

Above: The Battle of Jarama, February 1937.

to bombing sorties on them by the Legion's Ju 52s and it was clear that the battle was in stalemate. Nevertheless, the Republicans counter-attacked in force on the 17th, striking towards Pingarrón in the south and in the north crossing the Manzanares river, a tributary of the Jarama, to take La Maranosa. Both attacks failed and the Republican forces suffered severe losses, particularly around the latter high ground, where the Legion's bombers were again deployed to blunt the onslaught. The fighting died away in the final days of February with the rival forces digging in to protect the ground they held. Jarama also confirmed the Legion's shortcomings. Faced with superior Soviet fighters, K/88's Ju 52s were quickly forced to abandon daylight support missions and the He 51 fighters supposedly protecting them were clearly shown to be outclassed. Indeed, only one of their pilots, Unteroffizier Hans-Jürgen Hepe, claimed victory over an enemy fighter throughout the whole of February. In response to this poor performance J/88's He 51s were ordered to abandon their bomber-escort role and concentrate on ground-attack missions on quieter sectors of the Madrid front.

Both sides had suffered high casualties along the Jarama, particularly among their best troops, yet Franco was still determined to continue his offensive operations. The Nationalists made a third attempt to isolate and capture the capital in March but this time from the northeast spearheaded by 30,000 recently deployed Italian troops that had been positioned to the south of the town of Siguenza with the intention of taking Guadalajara on the Madrid-Zaragoza road. The original plan had been to launch this force, which was supported by significant quantities of tanks and artillery as well as 50 fighters, towards Guadalajara in concert with the Jarama attack but the Italians had been fighting around Malaga in the south and bad weather delayed their transfer to the Madrid

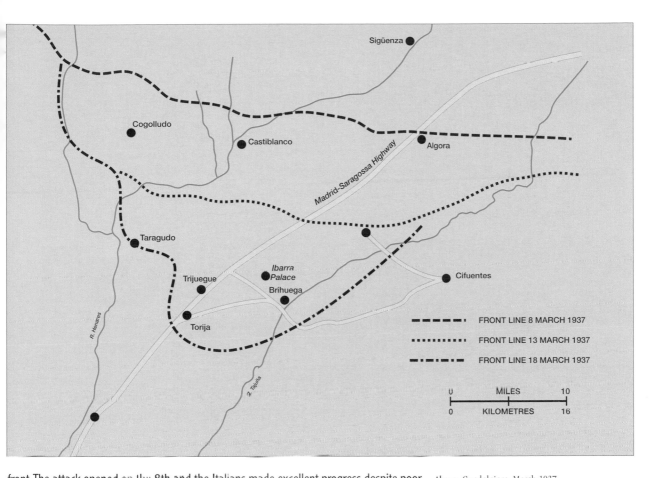

Above: Guadalajara, March 1937.

front. The attack opened on the 8th and the Italians made excellent progress despite poor weather, particularly the assault towards Brihuega that was spearheaded by motorised troops led by light tanks and armoured cars. Thereafter, the momentum ebbed away. On the 9th a combination of worsening weather and Italian exhaustion slowed the attacks, giving the Republicans time to rush reserves to the front. On the 10th the Italians took Brihuega and pushed closer towards Torija but then ran into Republic reinforcements. Two days later these troops launched a limited counter-attack with Russian T-26 and BT-5 tanks supported by several squadrons of Soviet fighters and Tupolev SB-2 Katiuska bombers leading the way. Unlike the Republican aircraft, which made use of concrete runways at Albecete, Nationalist aircraft was grounded by waterlogged airfields and was unable to support the hard-pressed Italians. Republican pressure intensified in the following days and reached a crescendo on the afternoon of the 18th, when the Republicans struck against Brihuega. A combination of poor Republican planning and the onset of night allowed the Italians to escape encirclement but the Battle of Brihuega was the Republic's first clear-cut victory of the war, one that was greatly to affect the Nationalists' war strategy. The Italian defeat would have been greater if it had not been for the low-level and bombing sorties flown by the Legion's He 51s and Ju 52s and the fire of F/88's flak batteries deployed in the ground role that slowed the Republican advance.

The collapse of the Italian-led attempt to capture Guadalajara highlighted the folly of Franco's previously unshakeable belief that the fall of Madrid would be swift and thus bring the civil war to a rapid resolution. The chief problem was that his forces were not only outnumbered by the Republicans but, apart from the Army of Africa, lacked the

training, experience or modern equipment to offset any quantitative imbalance between the two sides. Senior German officers had already begun to doubt Franco's strategy after the stalemate on the Madrid–Corunna road in December and had successfully demanded that Franco establish a joint German-Italian general staff to offer advice on war planning in January 1937. The failure to push across the Jarama Valley to sever the Valencia road the following month and the Battle of Brihuega convinced the staff members that not only were Franco's forces not up to the job but also the supposedly professional Italian contingent was far from a first-rate fighting force. They also saw that the Republicans, like Franco, recognised the symbolic importance of Madrid to the virtual exclusion and neglect of other fronts. Indeed, they had committed the best of their forces to the recent fighting demonstrated by the arrival of the Soviet-manned Polikarpov fighters, the deployment of the Russian-manufactured tanks that had proved far superior to their lightweight German and Italian counterparts and the commitment of the various International Brigades to the defence of Madrid. Their conclusion was stark: until the deficiencies of Franco's troops were rectified—and the Condor Legion's more advanced aircraft were available in quantity to win air superiority—the battle for Madrid would remain stalemated. Renewed attempts to take the great prize would only result in further severe Nationalist casualties. The staff concluded that the capture of Madrid should be abandoned and a new strategy implemented, one focused on overrunning more vulnerable Republican territories. They recognised that such a plan would undoubtedly prolong the civil war but such a situation would help distract the leading European powers from Hitler's plans for central Europe.

Left insert: German column. The suitcases identify this as an arrival or departure photograph — probably the latter: there are more images of the Legion leaving. *TRH Pictures*

Below: Republican soldiers and wounded at the battle of Brunete in July 1937. *TRH Pictures*

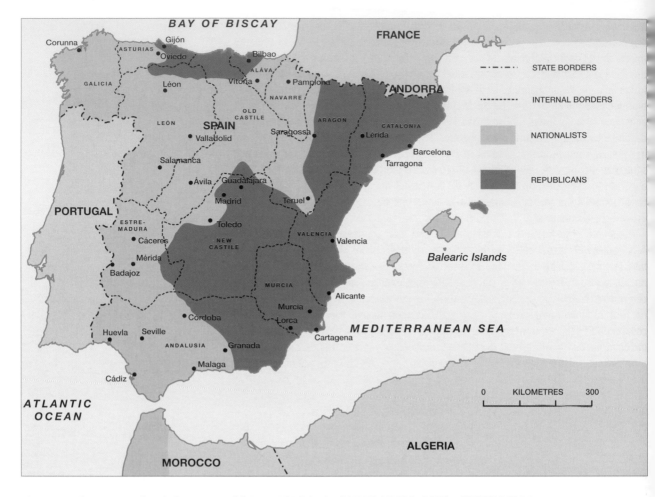

Above: By March 1937 Franco's forces had
consolidated their hold on the west of the country.

THE VIZCAYA CAMPAIGN AND GUERNICA

The most obvious target was the predominantly Basque province of Vizcaya, a valuable mining and industrial area along the peninsula's north coast that was isolated from Madrid by a broad swathe of Nationalist-held territory unlike the other major theatres in Aragon and Andalusia. The German members of the general staff also knew that the capture of the area's rich coal mines and steel plants would help fuel Nazi Germany's ongoing rearmament programme. Consequently, an attack on Vizcaya would not only be appropriate for their new strategy to win the civil war but would also neatly support Nazi Germany's own international aims.

The offensive against Vizcaya and its capital Bilbao was to be spearheaded by Spanish and Italian ground forces backed by Italian light tanks, all under the command of General Emilio Mola, but the offensive also saw the debut of the steadily re-equipping Staffeln of the Condor Legion. For their part, the Basques had a woefully small and largely outdated air force. Apart from a couple of squadrons of I-15s, they could call on the services of 27 Koolhoven FK-51 biplanes that were little more than basic trainers and 30 Avia A-101 biplane reconnaissance/bomber types that had been rejected as outdated by the Czech Air Force. Given the somewhat cool relationship between the autonomously minded Basque authorities and the Republican government, which was opposed to such calls for independence, the former could expect little outside help. The terrain also undoubtedly favoured the Condor Legion. The mountainous interior of the region left only a narrow coastal strip available for the Basques to build their airfields, thus making the Nationalist task of identifying their location easier, while the high ground masked the approach of Condor Legion aircraft approaching from the south and greatly reduced the time available for the Basque fighters to scramble. The Condor Legion assembled for the forthcoming operation in mid- to late March with its fighters based at Vitoria and its bombers situated around Burgos. Sperrle, the commander of the Legion, chose to remain at Franco's headquarters in Salamanca so actual command of the various squadrons devolved on his new deputy, Wolfram von Richthofen, who had arrived to replace Holle in January. Three squadrons of Ju 52 bombers, a squadron of He 111 bombers, three squadrons of He 51 fighters and half a squadron of Bf 109 fighters were initially available to von Richthofen but such was the paucity of the opposition's fighter force the He 51s were not required to protect the bombers and were quickly ordered to carry out ground-attack missions.

Mola launched his attack on March 31 with frontal assaults on three mountains—Albertia, Marota and Jacinto—on the southern edge of Vizcaya. The Condor Legion's bombers were deployed to attack Ochandiano to the immediate rear of the mountains and Durango, a town behind and some way to the north of the high ground that was a centre of road communications. Relays of Ju 52s rained bombs on Durango, which had no protecting anti-aircraft guns or indeed defenders of any type, and rubble from collapsed buildings quickly blocked the roads. The bombers killed a number of civilians, including 14 nuns and a priest holding a church ceremony. Most of the congregation also died. Follow-up strafing raids by He 51s that had little military justification against a defenceless town led to further non-combatant deaths and the Basques recorded that around 250 townsfolk died on the 31st. Most of the Basque front line collapsed over the following days in large part due to the close air support provided by relays of He 51s but the Nationalists did not capitalise on their early successes and halted their attacks on 4 April, the day that Ochandiano was captured. Subsequent operations were further delayed by bad weather and, although the Nationalists captured Durango and established positions just 20 miles (32 km) east of Bilbao, its was not until the latter part of April that they opened preliminary operations to prepare the way for the final offensive against Bilbao, which was protected by what the Basques had optimistically christened the Iron Ring. Before the Iron Ring could be tackled, the Basque front line had to be breached. Attacks began on the 20th and within five days the Basques were in full retreat toward Bilbao and its defences. The stage was now set for one of the most controversial events in the short career of the Condor Legion

Guernica was behind the fighting front and a communications hub through which any retreating Basque forces might withdraw. On the 26th at around 1630 hours the town's main church bells rang out briefly in alarm as Nationalist

Below: Battles around Bilbao, March–June 1937, showing the "Ring of Iron".

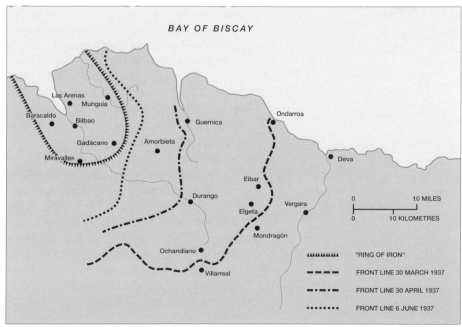

Above: A well-known photograph of He 111E 25 • 92 of 1.K/88 over Valencia. Note unit badge on tail fin (see pages 79–80 for more information on this badge). *via Austin Brown Photo Library*

aircraft were spotted. Townsfolk attending the weekly market took cover in cellars as a single Condor Legion He 111 of K/88 unleashed its bomb load on the town centre. After hearing the explosions above ground and the departure of the lone aircraft, the people emerged to help the wounded and survey the damage. However, the lone raider was merely marking the target and 15 minutes or so later the first of several waves of bombers struck Guernica. The locals returned to their cellars but many of these gave inadequate protection and the people abandoned them to seek sanctuary in fields and farmland around the town. As they did so they were strafed and bombed by the Legion's He 51s. For those on the ground who had survived these initial attacks, worse was to follow. At 1715 hours fresh waves of Legion bombers appeared in the skies over Guernica; this time three squadrons of Ju 52s carpet-bombed the target in relays for more than two hours. These aircraft carried a mixture of conventional high-explosive bombs, anti-personnel types and incendiaries that flattened the town and wrought havoc among the civilians present. Casualties totalled 1,654 dead and 889 wounded, roughly one-third of Guernica's peacetime population.

Despite incontrovertible evidence from numerous sources, including eyewitnesses and various foreign journalists who arrived shortly after the raid and identified fragments of German-made bombs amid the ruins, the Nationalists initially denied all responsibility for the attack, stating that the Basques themselves had destroyed the town and that none of their aircraft had flown on the day of the incident. Later, with the discovery of the metal fragments, they revealed that a few bombs had been dropped on Guernica but said that the bulk of the damage had been caused by Basque arsonists. On 4 May the Nationalist story changed yet again—that Guernica had been attacked over a period of a week by both artillery and aircraft, with the latter attacking infrequently over a single period of three hours, and had only suffered such severe damage after a prolonged ground and air bombardment. However, there is no doubt that the Condor Legion was solely responsible for Guernica. It is known that the Legion had been earmarked to attack Guernica, as von Richthofen recorded reaching such an agreement with the Nationalists on the 25th in his diary. Veterans later argued that the attack on the town was unplanned and unintentional, that the bombers were attempting to destroy the Rentaria bridge, a legitimate military target a little way outside Guernica, but that strong winds led their loads to overshoot the intended target. In his memoirs Adolf Galland, who did not arrive in Spain until the following July, added that the Legion's ineffective bomb sights and the crews' lack of experience had led to poor accuracy. While his justification contained an element of truth, the known facts tell a different story. There was little wind on the 26th, the German bombers attacked in line abreast rather than in a line-ahead formation that would have been more suitable for a raid on a bridge, and the mix of munitions, particularly the anti-personnel bombs and incendiaries, was inappropriate for such a small but solid structure. It seems most likely that the carpet-bombing of Guernica was undertaken as a military experiment to assess the potential of such raids not only to destroy urban areas but also to sap the morale of civilians.

Above: He 70s from Spanish Grupo 7-G-14. *via Austin Brown Photo Library*

Nationalist troops occupied what remained of Guernica on the 29th but subsequent ground attacks made only slow progress as the attack on the town appeared to have stiffened the resolve of the Basques to fight on. Whatever the truth of the matter, they conducted a successful fighting retreat into the Iron Ring. The Legion's bombers and ground-attack aircraft were frequently in action, yet it took the Nationalists until the end of May to reach the Iron Ring. Bad weather delayed the assault on these positions until 11 June by which time elements of the Legion had been sent south to Madrid to oppose an ongoing Republican offensive around Brunete. Nevertheless, the remaining elements of the Legion played a full role in the battle for Bilbao. When the main attack began south of the city on the 12th, three of F/88's batteries provided artillery support, while bombers and ground-attack aircraft flew dozens of sorties against the Iron Ring. By the end of the day it had been penetrated and the Basques finally surrendered Bilbao on the 19th. The fall of the town confirmed the indirect approach adopted at the suggestion of senior German liaison officers after the failure to capture Madrid was essentially correct and also demonstrated that the re-equipped Legion was vital to the Nationalist cause. The campaign had cost the Legion a mere eight aircraft and nine men had been lost in air combat, although 16 others had died in accidents or as a result of ground action.

THE BATTLE OF BRUNETE

By mid-May the ongoing fight for Vizcaya could no longer be ignored by the Republican authorities and, at the behest of the communists within the government, an offensive was planned against the town of Brunete, some 20 miles (32 km) west of Madrid. It was hoped that the attack would not only relieve some of the pressure on the Basques but also improve the Republican position around the capital. The Republicans committed some 50,000 troops to the assault at dawn on 6 July together with 140 aircraft, 128

tanks and some 220 artillery pieces. Their aim was to strike southward from the San Lorenzo del Escorial–Madrid road from a point northwest of the capital and capture the village of Brunete, thereby isolating the Nationalists besieging Madrid by severing their main west–east supply route. The Republicans caught the Nationalists by surprise, broke through their lines on a narrow front and occupied Brunete on the morning of the 7th but their assault prompted the immediate redeployment of Nationalist aircraft from the north to bases within easy reach of the battlefield. The Condor Legion's He 111s and Ju 52s regrouped at Salamanca, while the Bf 109s and Do 17s made for Avila. Both were little more than 30 minutes' flying time from the front, allowing the Legion to provide round-the-clock service over the battlefield.

The Nationalist air force made its presence felt from the 11th, the day the Republicans halted further attacks. Within two days around 75 percent of the Republican armoured vehicles had been destroyed or disabled as they made easy targets for both aircraft and artillery on the barren sun-baked plains where much of the fighting took place and the Republicans, still short of their final objective, dug in to hold the ground they had won at such cost. The Condor Legion was initially wary of participating in these ground-attack sorties, fearing that the enemy's large fighter force

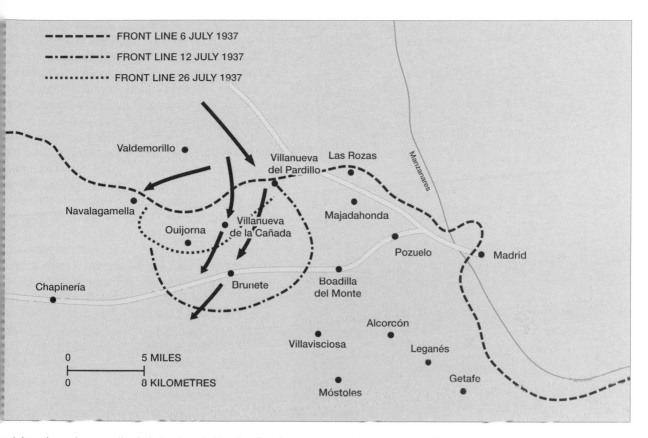

FRONT LINE 6 JULY 1937
FRONT LINE 12 JULY 1937
FRONT LINE 26 JULY 1937

Valdemorillo

Villanueva del Pardillo   Las Rozas

Manzanares

Navalagamella

Ouijorna   Villanueva de la Cañada   Majadahonda

Pozuelo   Madrid

Chapinería   Brunete   Boadilla del Monte

Alcorcón

Villavisciosa   Leganés

0   5 MILES
0   8 KILOMETRES

Getafe

Móstoles

Above: The battle of Brunete, June 1937.

Above Left: Pilots being briefed in front of Bf 109Ds. *TRH Pictures*

Left: 6 • 53, a Bf 109B of 2.J/88, seen during June 1937. It would be transferred to the Spanish Air Force rather than return to Germany. *via Chris Ellis*

might take a heavy toll of their aircraft. Yet the Republican fighters showed little aggressive spirit and Legion bombers and fighters were soon in action. Ju 52s and He 111s made both day and night attacks on Republican positions and the Bf 109s were committed in strength for the first time. On the 12th the Legion fighters recorded six victories—the highest tally in a single day to date —with Unteroffizier Guido Höness and Leutnant Rolf Pingel both scoring two kills. However, the former, whose two kills were a pair of Czech-built Aero A-100 light bombers, did not survive for long as he was in turn shot down by Frank Tinker Jr., a volunteer from the United States flying an I-16 whose eventual claim of eight victories made him the top-scoring American pilot of the conflict. Höness's Bf 109 was the first of its type to be confirmed downed but the new German fighters generally proved that they were superior to the Republic's I-15s and I-16s and Pingel confirmed the Messerschmitt's combat edge over its Soviet-built rivals by becoming the first Legion pilot to score five kills.

With the Republican ground assaults halted, the Nationalists took the offensive to recover the ground lost around Brunete, an area roughly eight miles (13 km) deep and 10 miles (16 km) wide. From the 18th, a day during which the Legion claimed 21 victories, they attacked high ground on both flanks and drove directly towards Brunete from the south. Legion medium bombers struck at Republican troop concentrations behind the front, while He 51s provided close air support for the Nationalist ground forces. The fighting was bitter but in part aided by German-supplied tanks and various anti-aircraft guns Nationalists finally broke through on the 24th, the day that a future Luftwaffe legend, Oberleutnant Adolf Galland, made his combat debut with 1./J/88. Brunete was recaptured the next day. Thereafter, the fighting ebbed away with the Nationalists regaining roughly two-thirds of the lost ground and Franco redeploying his forces to the far north with the intention of completing the occupation of Santander.

Brunete was a major setback for the Republic as it lost some 25,000 men, many from among its best units such as the International Brigades, and 100 aircraft compared with the Nationalists' 10,000 men and 23 aircraft. The Legion lost eight aircraft and nine men killed but 2./J/88 claimed 16 victories, with four going to Feldwebel Peter Boddem. The battle also highlights the value of German aid to Franco. Apart from demonstrating the effectiveness of the Condor Legion's newer aircraft, it also provided some valuable lessons for future German military theory. It was clear that the Republican armour had been used in ineffective penny-packets to support infantry attacks, while the Nationalists had deployed theirs en masse against key points of the front during the counter-attack thanks to the intervention of von Thoma. Although poorly armoured and lightly armed compared with the opposition, the Nationalist crews had to face few Republican tanks and anti-tank guns as many had been destroyed by air power in the first phases of the attack.

After the battle of Brunete, the Nationalists undertook the final conquest of northern Spain, returning to the offensive on 14 August. Backed by some 200 Condor Legion, Italian and Nationalist aircraft, Franco's ground troops swept forward under a protective cover of close-support aircraft while bombers ranged far behind Basque lines. The Italians met fierce resistance in the mountains but the Basques holding the Escudo Pass were finally forced to retreat under heavy aerial bombardment two days later. It was during this period that Condor Legion pilot Peter Boddem downed a further four Republican aircraft,

Above: Russian T-26B tanks armed with 37mm guns were supplied to the Republicans. *TRH Pictures*

Opposite, Above: Inside a Republican machine gun post at Jarama. *TRH Picture*

Opposite, Below: The battles around Santander and Asturias, August–October 1937.

bringing his tally to eight victories, the highest score of any Legion ace to date. Santander fell on the 19th but roughly half the remaining Basque forces escaped into the mountains of the neighbouring Asturias. The Nationalists pushed into the Asturias on 1 September, but the east-to-west advance was slowed by the difficult terrain. Nevertheless, the Legion's aircraft were in constant action—the He 51s in particular were flying up to seven ground-attack sorties each day, often attacking Basque positions from the rear. The defences finally crumbled during mid-October and the formal battle for the Asturias ended with the capture of Gijón, the capital, on the 21st, although the Basques waged a guerrilla campaign for a further five months. Clearing the Asturias had cost the Legion 12 aircraft and 22 men but its fighter pilots had chalked up 19 victories, eight of which were attributed to Oberleutnant Harro Harder. Vast quantities of ordnance had also been expended by the Legion to ensure victory, including 2,500 tons of bombs, more than one million rounds of machine-gun ammunition and some 22,000 8.8 cm shells.

The Nationalist victories in Vizcaya and Asturias of March–October 1937 ultimately proved decisive for the outcome of the civil war. They confirmed Franco as the unchallenged head of the various factions of the Spanish right and left him in control of some two-thirds of the country. Vizcaya and the Asturias also yielded iron and steel mills to the Nationalists. Much of the credit for the successes lay with the Condor Legion. Its bombers had pounded Nationalist positions, causing panic and destruction at will; its dive-bombers and ground-attack aircraft had struck targets with considerable precision, while its fighters had first swept the skies of enemy fighters and then strafed the enemy

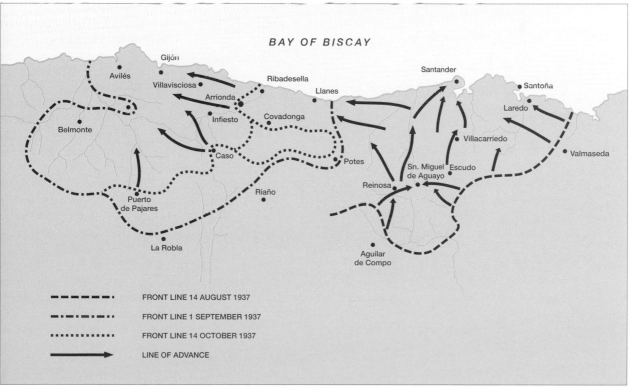

BAY OF BISCAY

Gijón
Avilés
Villaviciosa
Ribadesella
Llanes
Santander
Santoña
Arrionda
Laredo
Infiesto
Covadonga
Belmonte
Villacarriedo
Caso
Potes
Valmaseda
Sn. Miguel de Aguayo
Escudo
Reinosa
Puerto de Pajares
Riaño
La Robla
Aguilar de Compo

FRONT LINE 14 AUGUST 1937

FRONT LINE 1 SEPTEMBER 1937

FRONT LINE 14 OCTOBER 1937

LINE OF ADVANCE

with demoralising impact. Yet Franco had to pay a price for the Legion's aid—German engineers and contractors quickly took over many of the region's industrial and mining concerns and their output was sent to Germany to fuel its rearmament programme. The end of the Asturias campaign also saw changes within the Condor Legion. Sperrle returned to Germany at the end of October and his place was taken by Generalmajor Helmuth Volkmann. Von Richthofen continued to act as the Legion's chief of staff but following disagreements with Volkmann, he was eventually replaced by Major Hermann Plocher in early 1938.

TERUEL AND FALL OF ARAGÓN

After the conquest of northern Spain the Nationalists paused to review their strategic options for the next phase of the civil war. Both the German and Italian advisers wished to continue the indirect approach that had begun with the recent successes and, they believed, could be successfully continued with an invasion of Catalonia directed towards the occupation of Barcelona. In contrast, Franco believed that Catalonia was too well defended and that Madrid was a more realistic target. As the two camps debated the likely strategic options, the Condor Legion established a base at Soria and on 8 December 1937, began a short-lived campaign to destroy Republican airfields. This effort was prematurely halted a week later when the Republicans launched a pre-

Below: The position of the two sides in October 1937.

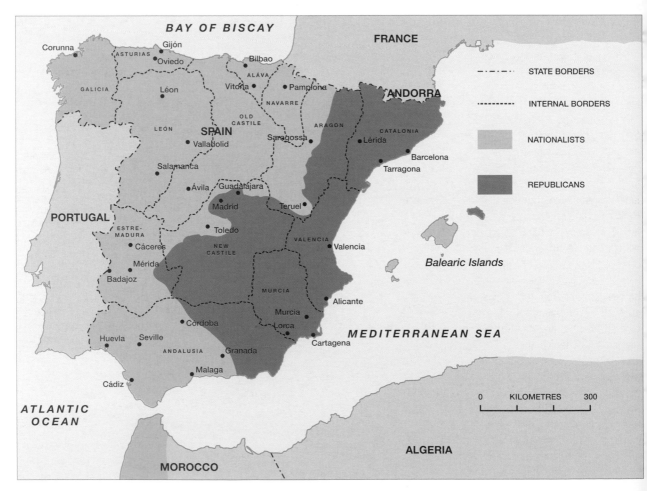

emptive ground strike against Teruel, a town in southern Aragon just 110 miles (180 km) south of Soria. While Franco gathered his forces for a major counter-attack on the 29th, the Legion was thrown into the battle—two of its 8.8 cm Flak batteries were immediately sent into action and its headquarters moved to Bronchales, a mere 25 miles (40 km) northwest of Teruel. Freezing conditions, snowstorms and poor visibility reduced the Legion's few aircraft able to get airborne to ground-support and interdiction missions that were unable to prevent the fall of the town on 6 January 1938.

Eleven days later, after an improvement in the weather, the Nationalists renewed their counter-attacks. Supported by massed artillery the drive towards the town smashed into the weakened Republican lines and, although they buckled, a decisive breakthrough proved elusive. Rather than continue a direct attack, the Nationalists attempted to capture Teruel by outflanking the position by way of the Alfambra valley, some 15 miles (24 km) to the north. For four days before the attack on 7 February the whole Legion softened up the inexperienced troops that held the Alfambra. Up to 100 sorties a day were launched and in the 24 hours before the ground offensive the Legion's aircraft dropped 120 tons of bombs on the enemy. On the 7th, as the Republican defences crumbled, the Legion's pilots engaged in fierce air battles and shot down two Republican fighters and 10 bombers. Four bombers fell to one pilot, Oberleutnant Wilhelm Balthasar, in a mere 10 minutes while Oberfeldwebel Reinhard Seiler claimed a further two. After breaking through along the Alfambra, the Nationalists immediately swung south towards Teruel, and it was during these attacks that the Legion deployed the Junkers Ju 87A for the first time. Three commanded by Leutnant Hermann Haas had arrived for evaluation in January and, after undertaking their first operation on 17 February, they soon proved to be extremely accurate when dive-bombing Republican targets. Teruel, or what little remained of it, was recaptured on the 22nd and the battle had proven a disaster for the Republicans, who suffered around 60,000 casualties and lost vast quantities of irreplaceable equipment. The Legion confirmed its domination of the skies, losing only five aircraft and 10 dead over the entire period.

Teruel proved a major springboard for the Nationalists. On the 24th—and much to the relief of his German advisers—Franco abandoned plans for the offensive on Madrid and opted, as they wished, to sweep the enemy from Aragon, attacking from east to west towards the Mediterranean, a move that, if successful would isolate Catalonia to the north from other Republican-held areas. The latter's capture would deliver a mortal blow to the Republic as Catalonia was a key industrial area into which war supplies flowed over the French border. The offensive opened on 9 March and, preceded by a massed artillery bombardment from more than 400 guns and ground-attack and bombing sorties from the Legion, the broad-front offensive, which began south of the Ebro, swept all before it. On the first day alone Moroccan troops, supported by tanks and the bombers of K/88 which dropped 88 tons of bombs in two massed raids, advanced some 25 miles (40 km). Much of the initial fighting was concentrated around the small town of Belchite, where the Legion's 8.8 cm guns as well as tanks manned by German personnel helped the Nationalists to cut through the Republican positions with considerable ease. Within 10 days the Nationalists had pushed the

Above: General der Flieger Hellmuth Volkmann was the second commander of the Legion from November 1937 to November 1938. *via Brian L. Davies*

Below: The Ju 87A arrived operationally in Spain in January 1938. The emblem carried on the undercarriage is a bowler hat and umbrella identifies Stukakette 88. *via Austin Brown Photo Library*

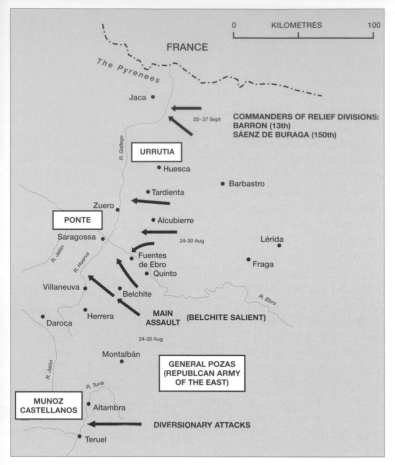

Republicans back between 30 and 60 miles (48–96 km) all along the front south of the river.

On the 22nd the focus of the offensive switched to the north, from the Ebro to the town of Huesca, and most of the Legion was redeployed to support these attacks towards the Segre river. Bitter fighting took place around Lérida and the Legion's 3./J/88 suffered two casualties, when aircraft flown by Hauptmann Hubertus Hering, the Staffel's commander, and Leutnant Manfred Michaelis collided over Alcarraz on the 30th. Galland replaced Hering as commander of the Staffel until May, when he in turn was replaced by Oberleutnant Werner Mölders, the officer destined to become the Legion's top-scoring ace. Despite such minor Nationalist setbacks, the Republicans were unable to mount a co-ordinated defence against these successive hammer blows and on 15 April Nationalist troops reached the Mediterranean coast at Vinaroz.

With Catalonia effectively isolated, the Nationalists concentrated their forces for an attack southward towards Valencia to complete the occupation of Aragon and further isolate Catalonia. The Legion established new bases, with its two-engined aircraft concentrated at Zaragoza and its one-engined types at various airfields around Vinaroz, including La Cenia from where J/88 operated and Benicarlo, which became the new headquarters. During May and June the Nationalists pushed on to Valencia aided by three of the Legion's 8.8 cm batteries and one of its 2 cm batteries but much to their surprise the Republicans opposing them did not collapse as they had done in recent battles. Terrain that favoured the defenders played its part in the slow Nationalist advance as did a resurgence in Republican air activity that was highlighted by raids on both La Cenia and Benicarlo in the first two weeks of June, but the weakness of the Condor Legion also played a part. Its bombers and Stukas supported the ground-attacks — K/88 dropped 56 tons of bombs on 5 June, for example — but the Legion's rapidly diminishing roster of serviceable aircraft was beginning to ring alarm bells among the staff. The figures were stark; it had lost some 20 percent of its strength, including 20 aircraft destroyed and seven badly damaged, since March and by 10 June only 30 Bf 109 fighters were available. Some senior officers believed they were being denied replacements as the Luftwaffe was on standby because of the looming crisis over Czechoslovakia but, whatever the truth of the matter, some new fighters had reached Spain by early July and were used to re-equip Mölders' 3./J/88. However, these had little opportunity to contribute to the stalemated battle for Valencia for within a matter of two weeks or so the Republicans launched their last great offensive of the civil war.

THE BATTLE OF THE EBRO

After the Nationalist capture of much of Aragon, the crucial sector of the front line followed the southern reaches of the Ebro between Lérida and the river's entry into the Mediterranean. It was here that the Army of the Ebro launched the Republic's biggest offensive of the war on the night of 24-25 July with the intention of forcing the Nationalists to abandon their push on Valencia and possibly reuniting the two Republican-held areas of Spain. A key objective was the town of Gandesa, a key communications centre some way to the west of the Ebro in the centre of the battle zone. A/88's Do 17s had spotted the build-up of Republican forces on the north bank of the river. Volkmann had become increasingly alarmed and on the 23rd the Legion's operations officer, Hauptmann Torsten Christ, informed the Nationalists that they could expect an imminent attack over the Ebro towards Cadensa, yet his concerns were ignored. Consequently, the Republicans crossed the Ebro at several points between Mequinenza and Cherta using pontoon bridges and achieved local surprise. The Nationalists were pushed back several miles in the first few days yet, crucially, the Republican forces could not take Gandesa and, as they battled to capture this important objective in the last week of July, Franco dispatched reinforcements, both ground and air units, to the front. The failure to take Gandesa owed much to the Legion, which flew an unprecedented number of missions between 25 and 31 July with the 70 or so aircraft at its disposal. K/88, A/88 and the Stukas made 664 sorties over this period and dropped around 689 tons of bombs. The bombers bore the brunt of this effort (422 sorties to deliver 486 tons of ordnance) and the main objectives were six bridges over the Ebro used by the Nationalists, which accounted for 322 of the total bombing raids. Although damaged frequently, they were never totally destroyed by the raids and were often repaired at night by Republican engineers.

With the momentum of the Republican attacks ebbing away, Franco went on the offensive on 6 August unleashing his troops in the northern sector of the front between Mequinenza and Fayon. This area was captured by the 7th, establishing a pattern that Franco would adopt for the remainder of the battle. A small sector of the Republican front would be pulverised by intense artillery and air strikes, killing or demoralising the Republican defenders, and then Nationalist ground troops would advance to occupy the position. Throughout August, September and October, the Nationalists nibbled away at the Republican lines, first striking in one

Left: The advance into Aragon, August–October 1937.

Below Left: The Battles around Teruel, December 1937–February 1938.

Below: The Aragon campaign, March–July 1938 showing Republican losses.

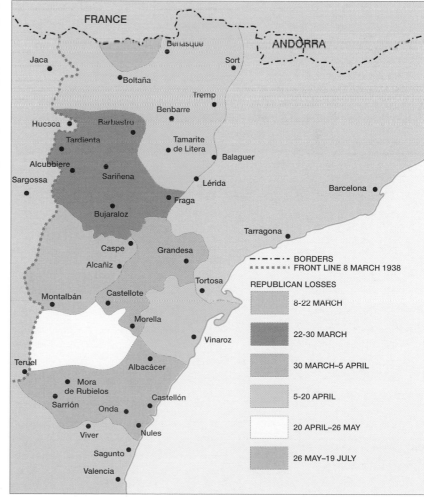

FRANCE
Benasque
ANDORRA
Jaca
Sort
Boltaña
Tremp
Benbarre
Huesca
Barbastro
Tamarite
de Litera
Tardienta
Balaguer
Alcubierre
Sargossa
Sariñena
Lérida
Barcelona
Fraga
Bujaraloz
Tarragona
Caspe
Grandesa
Alcañiz
Tortosa
Montalbán
Castellote
Morella
Vinaroz
Teruel
Albacácer
Mora
de Rubielos
Sarrión
Castellón
Onda
Viver
Nules
Sagunto
Valencia

– · – · – BORDERS
······ FRONT LINE 8 MARCH 1938
REPUBLICAN LOSSES

8-22 MARCH

22-30 MARCH

30 MARCH–5 APRIL

5-20 APRIL

20 APRIL–26 MAY

26 MAY–19 JULY

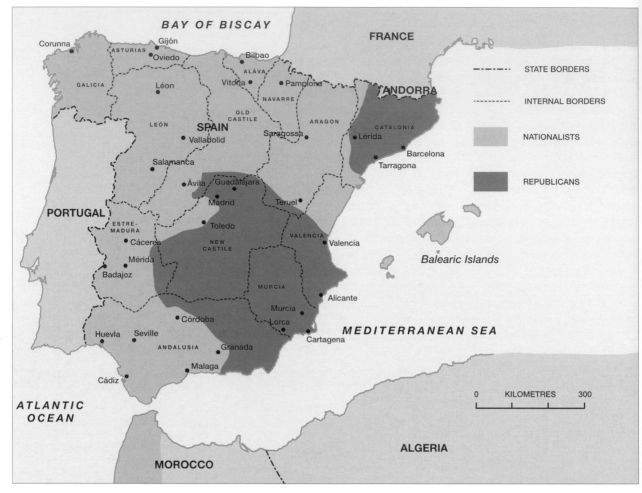

Above Left: The state of the two sides in July 1938.

Below Left: Republican troops in action in a cemetery on the Cordoba Front. *TRH Pictures*

Above: Russian maxim guns were used by the Republican troops in Spain. This photograph is circa 1937. *TRH Pictures*

Below: El Campesino directing Republican soldiers at Villanueva (see box page 45.). *TRH Pictures*

sector, making small gains, and then turning their attention elsewhere. However, events beyond Spain affected the Legion's efforts during September. As the international crisis over Czechoslovakia intensified, Volkmann was ordered to return some 250 of his aircrew to Germany, where the Luftwaffe was short of experienced men. At a stroke he lost 50 percent of his bomber crews and fighter pilots as well as 25 percent of his reconnaissance and seaplane crews. As a stopgap, a handful of trained Spaniards made up some of the shortfall; K/88's strength was bolstered by nine full crews. All of these replacements proved valuable but the intervention from Berlin led Volkmann to send off a highly critical letter to his superiors in mid-September that would lead to his recall in November.

The Nationalists launched a final offensive on 30 October. It was directed against the southeast section of the front and the opening daylight advance, which struck against the Sierra de Caballs, was followed by a nighttime push on the nearby Sierra de Pandols. Unprecedented levels of artillery fire were brought to bear on the Republican positions and the Nationalist air forces, including the Legion, hit the enemy hard. Five newly-arrived Ju 87Bs went into action for the first time and added their weight to the assaults. Within 72 hours the Nationalists reduced the Republic's remaining front-line aircraft strength by some 25 percent and by the end of the first week of November the Nationalists had retaken the whole area. Mölders claimed his 14th and last kill in Spain on the 3rd and one of his colleagues, Walter Oesau, who had arrived the previous April and had been steadily building up a considerable score, also claimed his ninth and last victory until World War 2 on the same day. The Republican command ordered a wholesale withdrawal back over the Ebro, which ended on the 16th. The 113 days of fighting along the river had ultimately proved a triumph for Franco; his forces had inflicted some 70,000 casualties on the Republicans between July and November, destroyed tons of irreplaceable supplies and equipment and swept the skies of enemy aircraft. The Legion had contributed greatly to his victory through its ground-attack, bombing and fighter sorties. Perhaps its greatest contribution was against the Ebro bridges which were targeted by a total of 1,600 sorties that dropped 1,713 tons of bombs on them. Yet for all this effort, Legion casualties were remarkably light. Records show that 10 aircraft had been destroyed, most in accidents rather than through enemy action, while another 14 had been badly damaged. Personnel losses were also trifling with only five aircrew killed, seven wounded and six captured. On the plus side, the Legion had accounted for around 100 Republican aircraft, a third of the total destroyed during the Ebro fighting, and 42 of the German kills were the work of Mölders' 3. /J/88.

The Legion was temporarily withdrawn from combat after the completion of the Nationalist counter-attack along the Ebro to allow its personnel some much-needed rest and to integrate new batches of aircraft into its

Below: The Ebro campaign, July–November 1938.

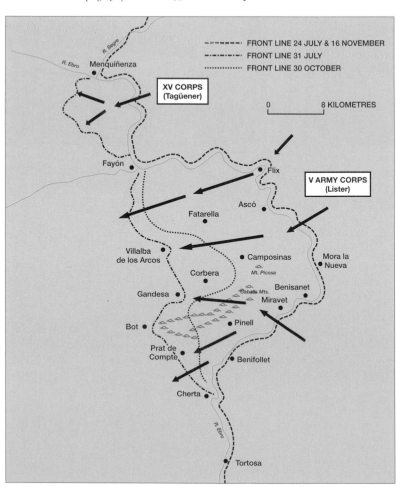

Staffeln. The new aircraft, which included Bf 109Es, He 111Es and Js and Hs 126As, brought its front-line strength up to 96, roughly 20 percent of the Nationalists' total air power. Fresh crews also arrived from Germany and the Spaniards temporarily attached to the Legion were returned to their parent units. The Legion also received a new commander following the departure of Volkmann in November; on 1 December von Richthofen arrived in Spain to take charge and was accompanied by a new chief of staff — Oberstleutnant Hans Seidemann.

Above: Republican forces during the Ebro campaign. *TRH Pictures*

THE FINAL BATTLES

After the successful conclusion of the Ebro counteroffensive in mid-November, Franco turned his attention towards Catalonia but hopes of a swift return to the attack were dashed because of thick fogs and heavy rains. The offensive into Catalonia finally began on 23 December and involved three main thrusts towards the cities of Barcelona, Gerona and Tarragona from the Ebro. Despite often appalling weather, the Legion played a full part in the offensive, launching an average of four sorties each day. Apart from the usual ground-attack missions against Republican troops and bombing raids on key lines of communications, its chief role was to finish off the enemy's remaining air force, which was estimated at around 106 aircraft of all types but only 50 percent of which were probably serviceable because of a lack of spares. The Legion sought out the Republican aircraft with considerable success, particularly during January and February 1939. On January 12 K/88 bombers wrecked 10 aircraft on the ground at Monjos and Pate, while J/88 fighters destroyed or badly damaged 26 aircraft during an attack on Vilajuiga airfield on 6 February.

The Nationalist advance was by now in full flow and the troops met little opposition as they pushed towards the Pyrenees and the border with France. Villages and towns fell

El Campesino

Valentin Gonzalez, known as *El Campesino* (The Peasant), was the commander of one of the Mixed Brigades and fought in all the major battles of the war, especially around Madrid at Brunete and then at Corunna Road (December 1936), Guadalajara (March 1937), Aragón (August–October 1937), Teruel (December 1937–February 1938) and in the Catalan campaigns in 1938. One of the most successful Republican commanders of the war, he was known for his brutal use of prisoners. He fled to the Soviet Union in 1939 but quickly became disillusioned there and went to live in France where he died in 1965.

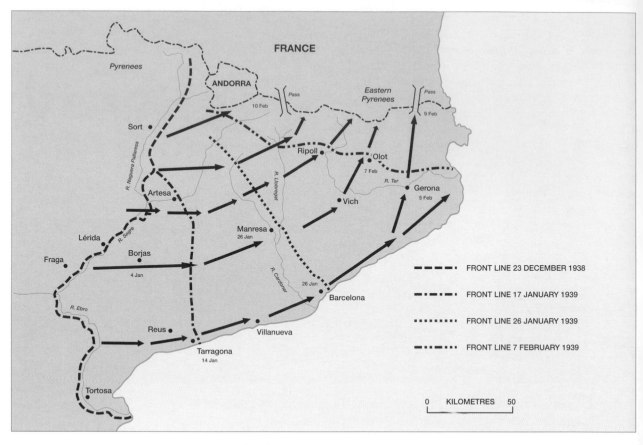

Above: Battles in Catalonia, December 1938–February 1939.

with barely a shot fired and on 14 January Franco's troops captured Tarragona. Two weeks later Barcelona, the Catalan capital, fell and on February 5 the Nationalists entered Gerona. Three days later they occupied Figueras close to the border with France, effectively bringing the campaign to an end. For its part, the Legion had suffered remarkably few casualties with 21 aircrew killed together with ten other men from F/88 and Ln/88. Eleven aircraft were also lost.

After the Catalan campaign, the Legion took part in a major parade in front of Franco in Barcelona on 21 February and then transferred to central Spain for the expected final offensive to capture Madrid. A new headquarters was established at Toledo and the Legion continued to see action against the few Republican aircraft that remained operational. On 5 March the Legion scored its final air victory—a Polikarpov I-15 shot down in a dogfight over Alicante by a Bf 109 flown by Oberleutnant Hubertus von Bonin, Mölders' replacement as head of 3./J/88 who had already notched up three kills. The German fighters continued to sweep the skies over the following days but no opposition was met. The Legion's reconnaissance and bombing units were kept busy but it was clear that Republican resistance was crumbling fast. On 26 March, the day that the Nationalists planned to launch their great final offensive against the capital, the Republican government accepted the inevitable and agreed to Franco's terms of unconditional surrender—there would be no battle for Madrid.

Franco's swift victory in the spring of 1939 heralded the rapid dissolution of the Condor Legion but not before it had taken part in several victory parades. The first, in Seville on 17 April, was followed by a second at Valencia on 3 May and a third at Barajas on 12 May. Seven days later the Nationalists held a huge march through the centre of Madrid in which the Legion participated and this was followed by a farewell parade at

Leon three days later. From there, the German volunteers headed westward for the port of Vigo on the northwest coast. On the 24th several German civilian vessels anchored in the harbour to unload 700 tons of humanitarian aid for Spanish civilians and then transport the men home. Among these were *Der Deutsche, Oceana, Robert Ley, Sierra Cordoba, Stuttgart* and *Wilhelm Gustloff*—most were liners of the *Kraft durch Freude* (Strength through Joy) organisation ostensibly established by the Nazis to provide the German working class with affordable holidays. Two days later 281 Legion officers and 4,383 men as well as 412 civilian technicians embarked for the sea journey home. Also on board were some 700 tons of equipment as well as many of the Legion's most up-to-date Bf 109s, He 111s and Ju 87s; most of the remainder of their equipment was left behind and bought by the Nationalists. Arriving at Hamburg on the 30th, the returnees were escorted into the port by several warships, including *Admiral Graf Spee* and *Admiral Scheer*, and were greeted by Göring on their disembarkation. On 6 June they and previously returned veterans, around 14,000 legionnaries in total, were honoured by a parade through Berlin in the presence of Hitler—the final public act of their brief career as an expeditionary force.

Around 19,000 Germans participated in the civil war but by no means all of these served with the Legion, which had an average strength of around 6,000 men, as many of the remainder were instructors or civilian experts. Although the records are not wholly accurate, the German pilots shot down over 320 Republican aircraft or destroyed them

Below: By February 1939 the Republicans were barely holding onto Madrid and the southeast of Spain.

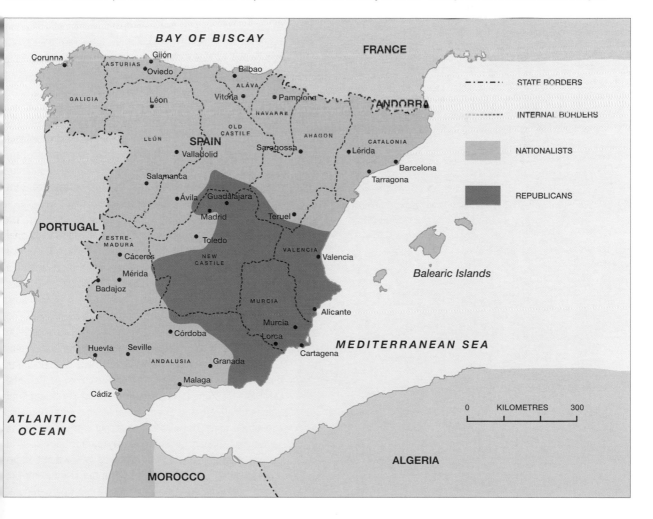

on the ground and the Legion's anti-aircraft batteries accounted for a further 59. The bombers of K/88 dropped around 21,000 tons of ordnance in support of the Nationalists and the Legion's aircrews also claimed to have sunk 60 ships of various types. On the debit side 72 German aircraft, including 15 bombers and 42 fighters, were destroyed by the Republicans but a further 160, including 39 bombers and 78 fighters, were written off in accidents—a substantial rate of loss for a comparatively small force. The Legion recorded 298 deaths during the civil war but of these just 178 were in action while 120 succumbed to non-combat accidents or illness. A further 139 men were wounded by the enemy, a figure dwarfed by the 449 men accidentally injured. The human and material loss was matched by a financial price, with the intervention costing Nazi Germany more than 500 million Reichsmarks. Of this, some 88 million had been spent on various salaries and expenses, which the Spanish did not have to repay, and a further 124 million was swallowed up on supplies to aid the Nationalist war effort. The remainder, and greater part of the total, some 354 million, was directly attributable to maintaining the Condor Legion itself. Germany extracted a price for sending the Condor Legion to Spain. The appropriation of the output of Basque iron and steel mills has already been mentioned and shortly before the beginning of the Catalan campaign, Franco agreed to sign an additional agreement that gave Germany rights over the output of five mines on the Spanish mainland and one in Spanish Morocco. He had little choice—if he had not agreed to what became known as the Montana Project he would in all likelihood have lost the Legion's invaluable support in the war's final campaign.

AUFKLÄRUNGSSTAFFEL SEE 88

Although the Condor Legion's aircraft were predominantly land based, it also included one detachment that conducted maritime operations. Known as *Aufklärungsstaffel See* 88 (AS/88—Maritime Reconnaissance Staffel 88), it operated independently against enemy shipping, ports, and coastal communications, but also supported ground offensives by sometimes striking far inland such key positions such as bridges. Floatplanes were first deployed to Spain in October 1936, when a small number of two-man Heinkel He 60s began operating from Cadiz to protect German shipping

bringing supplies to the Nationalists. However, within a few days these carried out their first major combat mission, attacking Republican aircraft docked at Malaga together with Ju 52s and He 60s. The creation of the Condor Legion led to the establishment of a small floatplane unit under Major Karl-Heinz Wolff. Initially AS/88's two He 60s and two Heinkel He 59s acted largely as the eyes of the small Nationalist navy but from January 1937, following a move from Cadiz to Melilla in Spanish Morocco the previous December, its He 59 four-man floatplanes began operating with torpedoes. On the 30th one pilot, Oberleutnant Werner Klümper, was able to torpedo and badly damage the cargo vessel *Delfin*. In mid-February 1937 AS/88 moved from Melilla to recently captured Malaga on the mainland. Here it received two new He 59s and a single He 60. However, Malaga was far from suitable as a base and the detachment moved once again, this time to the Bay of Pollensa on Majorca. From mid-June, when the Nationalists authorised attacks on all Republican ports so long as they contained no British ships, AS/88 began regular attacks on shipping and in the second half of the year attacked 10 vessels, sinking three and forcing two others to beach. However, the Norwegian aerial torpedoes being tested by AS/88 proved of poor quality and the floatplanes resorted to bombing and strafing targets.

AS/88's operations intensified further from January 1938 when Major Martin Harlinghausen its new commander

extended the unit's range of targets to include coastal communications. His aircraft either bombed targets or strafed them with the 2 cm cannon mounted in the nose of the He 59s. Harlinghausen also developed a new bombing tactic—aircraft approached the land at high altitude from seaward, cut their engines to glide to the target and then restarted them for a swift departure after bombing at very low level. The commander himself demonstrated this new tactic on the 19th when he accompanied an He 59 to Valencia and successfully bombed a large fuel dump from just 60 ft (50 m). Over the following months AS/88's range of targets included Alicante, Almeria, Barcelona and Cartagena, and Harlinghausen's steely determination to succeed as head of the unit earned him the nickname 'Iron Gustav'. As suitable naval and coastal targets became rarer, AS/88 also operated deep inland against bridges and rail lines and often at night to mask its slow-moving floatplanes from enemy ground fire and fighters. In November 1937 during the Battle of Teruel it attacked a suspension bridge over the Ebro at Amposta but scored only

Top: A Spanish sailor poses in front of an AS/88 He 59 in Pollensa. Note the 20mm in the nose. *via Patrick Laureau*

Above: The main moorings at Pollensa. On the land can be seen three He 60s. *via Patrick Laureau*

Opposite, Above: International Brigade members on the Ebro Front in 1938. *TRH Pictures*

Opposite, Below: Hermann Göring inspects returning Condor Legion troops. *TRH Pictures*

German Aircraft Deployed in Spain 1936–39

Type	Variants	Role	First Delivery	Total
Arado Ar 66	C	basic trainer	1939	6
Arado Ar 68	E	fighter	1938	3
Arado Ar 95	A	torpedo/reconnaissance seaplane	1938	9
Bücker Bü 131	A	basic trainer	1936	50
Bücker Bü 133	C	advanced trainer	1937	20
Dornier Do 17	E/F/P	medium bomber/reconnaissance	1937	27
Fieseler Fi 156	A	liaison	1938	6
Gotha Go 145	A	basic trainer	1938	21
Heinkel He 45	C	light bomber/reconnaissance	1936	47
Heinkel He 46	C	liaison/reconnaissance	1936	21
Heinkel He 50	G	dive-bomber/reconnaissance	1936	1
Heinkel He 51	B/C	fighter/ground-attack	1936	131
Heinkel He 59	B	torpedo/multi-role seaplane	1936	17
Heinkel He 60	E	reconnaissance seaplane	1936	8
Heinkel He 70	E/F	medium bomber/reconnaissance	1936	31
Heinkel He 111	B/E/J	medium bomber	1937	100
Heinkel He 112	V*/B	fighter/ground-attack	1936	10
Heinkel He 115	A	torpedo/multi-role seaplane	1939	2
Henschel He 123	A	dive-bomber/ground-attack	1936	17
Henschel He 126	A	liaison/multi-role	1938	6
Junkers Ju 52		medium bomber/transport	1936	116
Junkers Ju 86	D	medium bomber	1937	5
Junkers Ju 87	A/B	dive-bomber/ground-attack	1936	6
Junkers Ju W 34 hi		transport/multi-role	1936	5
Klemm Kl 32	A	liaison	1937	3
Messerschmitt Bf 109	V*/B/C/D/E	fighter	1936	133

*V denotes prototype.

Condor Legion Deaths in Spain 1936–39

Unit	Killed in Action	Accident	Sickness	TOTAL
Aufklärungsgruppe A/88	19	3	1	23
Aufklärungsstaffel See AS/88	11	4	1	16
Flakabteilung F/88	21	11	1	33
Jagdgruppe J/88	26	3	5	34
Kampfgruppe K/88	72	20	4	96
Nachtrichtenabteilung Ln/88	12	33	3	48
Naval	1	4	0	5
Panzerabteilung Imker	7	14	7	28
Stab S/88	3	5	0	8
Technical Services P/88	6	1	0	7
TOTAL	178	98	22	298

German Monthly Combat Deaths 1936–39 (1)

	1936	1937	1938	1939
January		11	4	18
February		5	1	5
March		3	8	6
April		10	10	
May		2	2	
June		16	3	
July		10	3	
August	2	2	2	
September	1	17	0	
October	0	5	5	
November	3	3	1	
December	5	8	6	
Total (2)	11	92	45	29

1) These figures include all deaths among troops engaged in active operations, specifically those who were killed in action by enemy fire, crashes, premature explosion of ordnance, mechanical failure or accident.

2) The grand total of 177 deaths excludes one senior NCO, Obergefreiter Gerhard Imping of Stab S/88, whose details are lost.

near-misses. However, on March 10, 1938, the unit returned to the target and sent its central section crashing into the river. Such efforts to support Nationalist ground operations became the mainstay of AS/88's workload until the end of hostilities in 1939.

Both Wolff and Harlinghausen received the Spanish Cross in Gold with Swords and Diamonds for their leadership of what was one of the Legion's smallest units. AS/88 recorded 11 men killed in action, most in 1938 during ground-support operations in Catalonia. Three were killed when their aircraft exploded in mid-air over Cambrils on 21 March and a further five died on 31 December when their aircraft was shot down over Valls. Apart from combat deaths, five others succumbed to illness or were involved in fatal accidents, including the four men who died on 1 January, 1939, when their aircraft crashed because of heavy icing.

Above Left: Do 17 of the period—the serial (54 • D12) is not one of the Condor aircraft. *via Austin Brown Photo Library*

Right: He 45 15 • 20 in Leon November 1937: note unusual camouflage, green over grey, first used in this campaign. *via Chris Ellis*

Below Right: Bf 109B-1 of 1.J/88 (identified by white cross in the black fuselage cockade). *TRH Pictures*

Below: Bf 109B-1 • 6-7 after a crash landing by Feldwebel Norbert Flegel on La Albericia airfield. The aircraft was repaired and would be used by Werner Mölders of 3.J/88. The Top Hat marking identifies 2.J/88. *TRH Pictures*

Opposite, Above: Bf 109V5 • 6-3 was an early arrival in Spain (December 1936) and was flown by Oblt Hennig Strümpell with VJ/88 and then 2.J/88. *TRH Pictures*

Opposite, Below: Do 17 refuelling. *via Austin Brown Photo Library*

Right: Do 17E 27 • 23 of A/88 seen from the dorsal turrret of an accompanying aircraft. Note the emblem of a devil riding a bomb which would go on to be used by one of KG3's Staffeln in World War 2. 27 • 23 arrived in Spain in July 1938. *TRH Pictures*

Below Right: Lineup of He 51s. The serials show that these are not Condor Legion aircraft although of the same vintage. *via Austin Brown Photo Library*

Below: Hs 126 lineup. Few Hs 126 aircraft reached Spain: they were too slow to be effective on the modern battlefield. *via Austin Brown Photo Library*

Left: The rugged Polikarpov I-16 Rata saw widespread use in Spain on the Republican side. *TRH Pictures*

Below Left and Below: Two views of the Polikarpov I-15 Chato biplane. A modified version of this aircraft had established a world altiutude record of 47,818ft in November 1935. *TRH Pictures*

Above: Tupolev SB-2 bombers struck the
Deutschland on 29 May 1937. *TRH Pictures*

THE KRIEGSMARINE'S CIVIL WAR

Ostensibly, the Kriegsmarine was part of an international maritime force that was supposed to prevent outside supplies from reaching either the Republicans or Nationalists. The scheme began on 28 September, 1936, when Germany joined Belgium, Britain, Czechoslovakia, France, Italy, the Soviet Union and Sweden in signing a non-intervention agreement, yet for several of these countries, chiefly Germany, Italy, France and the Soviet Union, the accord was little more than a sham as they actively supported one side or the other. Indeed, the pocket battleship *Deutschland* had docked at Cueta in Spanish Morocco as early as 3 August, little more than two weeks after the outbreak of the civil war, and its senior officers had dined with Franco and a number of his Nazi advisers. Apart from escorting transport ships carrying war supplies and personnel to Spanish ports, the Kriegsmarine's surface warships took a much more active part in the civil war. Initially, they covered the transfer of the Army of Africa from Spanish Morocco to the mainland, and by mid-October the naval strength around Spain consisted of the pocket battleships *Deutschland* and *Admiral Scheer*, the light cruiser *Köln* and four ships of the 2nd Torpedo-boat Flotilla, *Albatros*, *Leopard*, *Luchs* and *Seeadler*. Twice during the first half of October 1936, these ships discovered the extent to which the Republicans were receiving secret aid from the Soviet Union. The *Luchs* sailed into Cartagena harbour and photographed the Russian transport ship *Komsomol* with a cargo of trucks on its deck, while on the 15th the steamer *Bolshevik* was also filmed with war materials on its decks. Such evidence helped convince Hitler to expand the German commitment to the Nationalists and over the following months the surface warships aided the transfer of Condor Legion aircraft from Germany to Spain by way of Italy. They operated radio beacons so that the aircraft could safely cross the Mediterranean and during this period the *Admiral Scheer* and the cruiser *Königsberg* each recovered a Heinkel He 59 floatplane that had been forced to land on the open sea. The Kriegsmarine also formed what was codenamed the 'North Sea Group', a body based on the *Deutschland* and *Admiral Scheer* consisting of personnel to train the Nationalists in various maritime skills, such as communications, gunnery, mine warfare and the operation of light naval forces.

The Kriegsmarine also took part in direct combat. During the first week of February 1937, the pocket battleship *Admiral Graf Spee* supported elements of the Nationalist fleet bombarding the port of Malaga, allowing Franco's forces to occupy the port on the 8th amid scenes of great brutality. The following April the same pocket battleship supported Nationalist warships off the northern coast of Spain when they stopped a British merchantman heading for the Republican-held Basque port of Bilbao. Only the arrival of two Royal Navy warships prevented the cargo vessel from being either boarded or sunk. On 29 May the Kriegsmarine suffered its greatest loss of life during the civil war when the *Deutschland* was attacked by two Republican SB-2 Katiuska bombers crewed by Russians while at anchor off Ibiza accompanied by *Leopard* and the tanker *Neptun*. Later claiming that they believed *Deutschland* to be the Nationalist flagship *Canarias*, the Soviet crews struck in the early evening with the sun hiding their approach. Three bombs were dropped and two hit the warship's deck. One pierced the armour and exploded in the seamen's mess, eventually killing 32 sailors and wounding a further 73. As the aircraft departed four Republican destroyers bombarded the Ibizan coast from a range of 10 miles (16 km), but without doing much damage.

The *Deutschland* was not put out of action by the raid but sailed for Gibraltar, where the casualties, both dead and wounded, were put ashore. Hitler, who received news of the attack while attending an agricultural show in Munich the following day, ordered an immediate response. He demanded that Valencia, the new seat of the Republican government, should be attacked but concerns about minefields in the area led to Almeria being selected instead. Shortly after dawn on the 31st the *Admiral Scheer* supported by the *Albatros*, *Leopard*, *Luchs* and *Seeadler* opened fire on the port. The attack lasted just 30 minutes until 0758 hours and some 250 shells of various calibres hit the port and its facilities causing considerable damage to buildings, several fires and left 19 locals dead. Republican shore batteries fired around 60 shells in reply but the warships withdrew without damage. While the events of April–May were taking place Germany remained party to an agreement signed by the members of the Non-Intervention Committee in March that required warships from Britain, France, Germany and Italy to patrol Spanish waters to prevent war supplies reaching either the Nationalists or Republicans. Hitler threatened to withdraw from the agreement after the attack on the *Deutschland* but British diplomacy delayed Germany's withdrawal. However, the German leader claimed that the cruiser *Leipzig* had been attacked off Oran, French Algeria, by an unidentified submarine on 15 and 18 June and used the events to withdraw from the international naval patrols.

Below: *Deutschland* burns following the air attack. *via Jak Mallmann-Showell*

Above: The dead are taken off board with full military honours. *via Jak Mallmann-Showell*

OPERATION 'URSULA'

The deployment of various surface warships was the most tangible evidence of the Kriegsmarine's involvement in the civil war but it also conducted much more covert operations. The most secretive mission began on 20 November 1936, shortly after Germany and Italy had formally recognised Franco as Spain's legitimate head of state. On that day a pair of Type VII U-boats, the *U-33* under Kurt Freiwald and Harald Grosse's *U-34*, slipped out of Wilhelmshaven—both the captains and their crews had been ordered never to reveal their role in an order issued by the *Oberkommando der Kriegsmarine* (OKM) on the 6th. The submarines were part of the *Saltzwedel Flotilla*, which had been formed on 1 September and named in honour of Reinhold Saltzwedel, a World War 1 ace who had sunk 111 Allied vessels in 22 patrols before being lost in the English Channel on 2 December 1917. After leaving German waters, the two U-boats painted out any identification signs and then sailed on separate routes through the English Channel before heading south. They entered the western Mediterranean by way of the Bay of Biscay and the Strait of Gibraltar on the night of 27-28 November and, after taking over from Italian submarines, began seeking out Republican vessels. Their ground-breaking patrol, which lasted until December, was conducted in the utmost secrecy. If any U-boat got into difficulty it was under orders to sail to the Sardinian port of La Maddelena and enter the base flying an Italian ensign. The operation was codenamed Operation '*Ursula*' after the only daughter of Karl Dönitz, the prime-mover in the creation of the Kriegsmarine's new submarine arm, and its day-to-day running rested with Konteradmiral Hermann Boehme, who remained in Berlin and

Left: Closeup of an He 60 taking off from a ship's catapult. A few of these aircraft were used by AS/88 and then passed onto a Spanish unit. *TRH Pictures*

Below: *Deutschland* taking on victuals: note the Ar 196 seaplane on the catapult.
via Jak Mallmann-Showell

Pocket Battleship Service in the Civil War, 1936–38

Name	Year	From	To
Admiral Graf Spee	1936	20 August	9 October
	1936–37	13 December	14 February
	1937	2 March	6 May
		23 June	7 August
	1938	7 February	18 February
Admiral Scheer	1936	24 July	31 August
		2 October	3 December
	1937	15 March	7 April
		9 May	1 July
		30 July	11 October
	1938	19 March	29 July
Deutschland	1936	24 June	30 August
		1 October	19 November
	1937	31 January	24 March
		10 May	16 June
	1937–38	5 October	10 February
	1938	1 August	15 August
		20 September	23 October

acted as the liaison officer between the U-boat captains and the OKM.

The two boats began their patrol of the western Mediterranean on the 30th with the *U-33* operating around Alicante between Cape Palos and Cape Nao and the *U-34* from Cape Palos to south of Cartagena. However, their operations were far from successful for several reasons. The U-boat captains were hamstrung by high-ranking paranoia about their mission being uncovered, problems in reaching agreement on what were and what were not legitimate targets and difficulties in communicating with their superiors. Even when targets were engaged, the German torpedoes usually malfunctioned. Finally, orders were issued that the secret patrols were to be discontinued from 10 December. It was as the two submarines began their voyage back to Wilhelmshaven that they scored their one and only success, although even this is a matter of debate as a subsequent Republican enquiry concluded that the sinking was the result of an internal explosion and not enemy action. The German version of events was somewhat different. As the *U-34* sailed off Malaga making for the Strait of Gibraltar on the 11th, a look-out spotted the Republican submarine *C-3* sailing some five miles (eight km) off the coast at 1400 hours. Grosse submerged his boat and fired a single torpedo that struck the *C-3* at around 1420. The hull split in two and the submarine sank rapidly claiming the lives of all but three of its crew. This action marked the end of Operation 'Ursula' and the two *Saltzwedel* boats were back at Wilhelmshaven by the end of the month. Although evidence is sketchy, it does appear that several submarines were sent to Spanish waters during mid-1937 but few details of their operations are known beyond the fact that they were also drawn from the '*Saltzwedel*' Flotilla. Those believed to have been involved were *U-25, U-26, U-27, U-28, U-31* and *U-35*. It is also known that five submarine commanders were awarded the Spanish Cross in Bronze without Swords on 6 June 1939.

Below: *Admiral Graf Spee* in May 1937.
TRH Pictures

Left: *Deutschland* crew clear the deck after action. *via Jak Mallmann-Showell*

Below: *Admiral Graf Spee* off Almeria. *via Jak Mallmann-Showell*

INSIGNIA, CLOTHING & EQUIPMENT

Above: *Der ADLER* colour cover special issue: Condor Legion at the front.

As the involvement of German forces in the Spanish Civil War was supposed to be kept secret, those who volunteered or were sent out to the conflict generally dispensed with both uniforms and insignia that would identify their nationality. Personnel tended to wear clothing and badges that were used by the Nationalists, although there was considerable latitude in what was actually worn and styles were modified. With regard to equipment, while there is information on what types of aircraft (see page 50) and heavy equipment Germany sent out to Spain, precise details of volume and shipment dates are hard to find, again due to the secrecy that revolved around the mission.

UNIFORMS

Those who were sent to Spain travelled in civilian clothes and on their arrival did not change into German uniforms to maintain the subterfuge but rather wore a plethora of items with most sourced locally. Some of the first arrivals were even given white uniforms and caps that had been worn by some police during the 1936 Olympic Games in Berlin, while tank personnel initially wore blue-grey overalls and a black Spanish beret. Undoubtedly, official German military clothing was worn, such as flying overalls and fatigues, but in general there was little standardisation and photographic evidence suggests that the men were allowed a considerable degree of latitude in what they wore when in action.

However, the German air and ground detachments did have an official service uniform. This consisted of a single-breasted tunic with four pockets in khaki-brown serge usually worn open-necked that bore a close resemblance to that produced by the Nationalists and probably originated from their stocks. Both officers and other ranks wore a khaki shirt and black tie with the tunic, and officers completed their uniforms with matching breeches and leather riding boots while other ranks tended to wear trousers with leather boots and, on occasion, puttees. Belts were also worn and came in two patterns: brown leather with a cross strap over the right shoulder for officers and a black belt without the shoulder strap for other ranks, who also wore y-strap webbing and ammunition pouches in combat.

Full kit was rarely worn as the summer heat led many to dispense with the tunic and wear the shirt with rolled up sleeves; in cold weather officers were often seen wearing German-style overcoats in blue-grey leather while a cloth version was issued to lower ranks. Tank crews wore overalls in various colours, including khaki and dark brown, with a large black Spanish beret. The most common form of headgear was similar to the Luftwaffe's Fliegermütze sidecap. Manufactured in khaki-brown cloth, this soft sidecap was officially worn by personnel up to the rank of Oberstleutnant (lieutenant-colonel) and insignia on the front identified the wearer's rank. More senior officers wore a peaked cap, also in khaki-brown, while in action some ground troops undoubtedly wore the German 1936 pattern steel helmet in blue-grey but again with no identifying insignia.

Below: Air badges: from top to bottom—Pilot; Pilot/Observer; Observer.

INSIGNIA AND BADGES

The men who served in Spain were temporarily promoted to one level above their normal rank but reverted back once they returned to Germany. To maintain the illusion that no Germans were involved in the civil war they wore rank badges that were based on those of the Nationalists, although there was considerable variation in their realisation. In the case of enlisted men and most officers rank badges were worn on the front of their sidecaps and on or above the tunic or shirt left breast pocket. For enlisted men gold-yellow bar(s) were worn horizontally on the breast and vertically on the sidecap, while junior officers wore one (Leutnant) or two (Oberleutnant) six-pointed silver stars in similar positions. More senior ranks carried one (Hauptmann), two (Major—see photo on page 64) and three (Oberstleutnant and Oberst) eight-pointed gold stars. Generals wore a four-pointed star with crossed devices. All of these insignia were edged in branch of service colours and among these were black for staff and command; gold-yellow for air force personnel; bright red for anti-aircraft detachments; and light brown for signal units. However, there does appear to be at least one exception to this general rule of no German insignia. Many of the tank personnel continued to wear the silver death's head insignia of the German panzer arm while in Spain with a swastika positioned beneath it.

   Apart from rank insignia, some Condor Legion members also wore additional badges. Befitting a conflict in which language skills were important, Spanish-speaking German interpreters were entitled to wear a diamond-shaped cloth badge on their right breast pocket or front of the sidecap. This consisted of a vertical bar of silver lace topped by a similarly coloured dot placed on a background cloth in the colour of the interpreter's branch of service. In the case of specialists, additional badges came in the form of various metal or cloth designs based on Spanish regular army badges that could be worn on the tunic or headgear respectively but only if they had been presented to the wearer by the Nationalists. Among the badges available were a Maltese Cross surrounded by oak leaves for medical staff, a circular flaming grenade for ordnance personnel, and a gold star surrounded by oak

Above: The Commander of the Legion Condor, Generalmajor von Richthofen (left), having arrived at Avila in his 'plane, receives the first detailed situation report from the Legion's Chief of Staff, Oberstleutnant Seidemann (centre) and the Commander of the fighting group, Major Nielson. *via Brian L. Davies*

Left: Major Nielson conferring with other officers and NCOs of the Legion. Note the two stars above his breast pocket and on his cap: these identify the rank of Major (Spanish *teniente coronel*). *via Brian L. Davies*

Opposite, Above Left: Von Richthofen photographed in the field. *via Brian L. Davies*

Opposite, Above Right: A final muster parade for some of the combat fliers of the Legion. Photograph taken in May 1939. *via Brian L. Davies*

Opposite, Below Left: NCOs and other ranks of the Legion parade in Spain before their departure for Germany. *via Brian L. Davies*

Opposite, Below Right: The Berlin parade, reviewed by Adolf Hitler, was led by Generalmajor von Richthofen together with the Legion's three previous Commanders. They are seen here marching through the Brandenburg Tor along the Charlottenburger Chausser. *via Brian L. Davies*

Above: German volunteers march to the quayside at Vigo in readiness for their departure by sea to Hamburg. *via Brian L. Davies*

Left: Men of the Legion Condor photographed during the Victory Parade held in Madrid on 19 May 1939. Note the Spanish Crosses on the right breast pockets of the two front men. See page 76 for information on medals and decorations. *via Brian L. Davies*

Opposite, Above: The special military parade held in the Berlin Lustgarten involved over 14,000 troops, which included 3,000 sailors from the Kriegsmarine and 1,000 men from the German Army. *via Brian L. Davies*

Opposite, Below: Serried ranks of Legionnaires march past Hitler. *via Brian L. Davies*

leaves for administrative staff members. Spanish air force wings were also worn by German flying personnel above the right breast pocket and came in silver wire on a cloth backing or as a clasp badge. The style changed during the civil war; from 1936 to 1938, they did not include the Spanish royal crown but did so subsequently. Additional devices also identified the wearer's role: pilots had two crossed propellers; bombardiers a crossed rifle and bomb; observers a star; and radio operators a pair of crossed lightning bolts.

Many Germans who served in the civil war were decorated for bravery or overseas service by the Nationalist or Nazi leadership during or after the war (see box for German awards, page 77) and in June 1939, a cuff title was instituted to commemorate those who had served in the German tank units and signals detachment. Worn on the right forearm, it comprised a 3.2 cm strip of red cloth with the title '1936 Spanien 1939' in Gothic lettering with gold metallic thread that was also used as edging above and below the lettering. The colours were those associated with the Nationalists and later became the state colours of Franco's regime.

ARMOUR

Germany shipped two versions of the Panzerkampfwagen I (PzKpfw I) to Spain, the A and B. The design was pioneered by Krupp in the early 1930s, whose initial drawings were based on an imported British Carden-Loyd Mark VI chassis and given the designation LKA1. With Krupp developing the chassis and Daimler-Benz the hull and turret, the fine tuning of the design, which gained the cover title of La S (*Landwirtschaftlicher Schlepper*/agriculture tractor), was completed in December 1933.

Opposite, Above: Typical markings on the front of a PzKpfw I during the Civil War.

Opposite, Bottom: The PzKpfw I had a two-man crew and was armed with two 7.92mm MG13s. Both Ausf A and B versions saw service; this photograph shows the Ausf B, identifiable by the four return rollers (the Ausf A had a shorter chassis and only three). *TRH Pictures*

Below: German armoured troops equipped with PzKpfw I Ausf Bs. *TRH Pictures*

Full-scale production of what was a vehicle initially considered to be essentially for training purposes was placed with Henschel and finally got underway in 1934. Two versions, the 1A La S and 1B La S, rolled off the production lines and in 1938 they gained their final titles following the introduction of a new code for tank designation. The PzKpfw IA weighed in at 5.4 tons and was 14 ft (4.6 m) long, 6 ft 10 in wide (2 m) and 5 ft 8 in (1.7 m) high. Power was provided by a four-cylinder petrol engine that generated a top speed of 23 mph (35 km/h). The tank was operated by a two-man crew (commander/gunner and driver) and was armed with a pair of 7.92 mm machine guns, either the older MG13 or, more commonly, the excellent MG34. The Mark IB version was given a larger, more powerful engine that necessitated an increase in the overall length of the vehicle and the addition of a fifth suspension wheel but increased the speed to 25 mph (40 km/h). Battle experience in the Spanish Civil War indicated that the PzKpfw I had several weaknesses. Its 0.5 in (13 mm) armour offered little protection against even the smallest anti-tank guns possessed by the Republicans; its weapons were far too lightweight to take on enemy tanks; the vehicle lacked the endurance to participate in prolonged

Top: The Spanien cuff-title was awarded to all those who served in Spain. Note the use of the commemorative honour title Legion Condor, awarded by Führerbefehl, on the sleeve of the officer in the photograph opposite.

Above: This is a ring made by Moroccan natives in Spain and sold to the members of the Legion in 1936. It is in silver with gold appliqué. It has an eagle and swastika with the LC logo of the corps and P/188 as the squadron. Below this is the word *España* (Spain).

Below: This artwork is of a sword presented by Otto Telshow, Gauleiter of East Hanover, to a returning legion member, Unteroffizier Friedrich Lindemann, who came from the district. The blade is by SMF Solingen and engraved in Spain. It reads: *Für unseren siegreichen Piloten Unteroffizer* [sic] *Friedrich Lindemann. Aus ihrer Heimatstadt Hannover Gauleiter Ost-Hannover.* (For our victorious pilot Unteroffizier Friedrich Lindemann from your home town Hannover.)

Far Left: Generalmajor Wolfram Freiherr von Richthofen, was the last Commander of the Legion Condor, November 1938 to May 1939. *via Brian L. Davies*

Left: Von Richthofen at the official reception for the troops of the Legion Condor held at Hamburg, their port of entry on their return to Germany, 31 May 1939. *via Brian L. Davies*

Below: Officers from the Luftwaffe fighter squadron, KG 53, plotting positions on a map from information received via wireless transmission. Note the 'Legion Condor' commemorative honour title being worn by the junior officer on the left. This particular cuff-title was instituted in June 1939. *via Brian L. Davies*

Top: 2cm Flack 30. *TRH Pictures*

Above: 88mm dual-purpose gun with halftrack prime mover. *TRH Pictures*

Opposite: Two views of the PzKpfw I—above an Ausf A; below an Ausf B. *TRH Pictures*

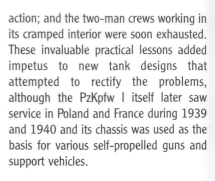

action; and the two-man crews working in its cramped interior were soon exhausted. These invaluable practical lessons added impetus to new tank designs that attempted to rectify the problems, although the PzKpfw I itself later saw service in Poland and France during 1939 and 1940 and its chassis was used as the basis for various self-propelled guns and support vehicles.

ARTILLERY

Although the Condor Legion was equipped with the 2 cm Flak 30 and 3.7 cm Flak 36 anti-aircraft guns and the ground units had 2 cm anti-tank guns, of greater significance was the 8.8 cm. This had been devised as a dedicated anti-aircraft gun by Krupp personnel working with Sweden's Bofors company in the late 1920s and a prototype was built shortly after the former returned to Germany in 1931. Immediately approved by the authorities, the weapon entered service two years later under the designation Flak 18. It was transported on two sets of detachable wheels and had a cruciform arrangement of legs that were deployed to maximise firing stability. The gun was capable of firing up to 15 rounds per minute under ideal conditions and the 21 lb (9.5 kg) shell could reach a maximum altitude of some 32,500 ft (9,900 m), although its effective ceiling was nearer 26,250 ft (8,000 m). Tests indicated that the weapon could also be deployed in a ground role with a maximum range of some nine miles (14.4 km). Further improvements were soon made to the basic design, most notably to the lining of the barrel and sighting mechanism, and the modified version, known as the Flak 36, entered service in 1937. Both types were deployed to aid the Nationalists and were initially used purely in the anti-aircraft role. Their ability to offer direct support to ground operations was soon apparent to some, although these capabilities were not fully recognised until the fighting in the Western Desert during World War 2.

TRANSPORT AND SUPPORT VEHICLES

One of the constant bugbears encountered by the Condor Legion in Spain was the lack of most types of such vehicles although various components were frequently moved from one theatre to another through the conflict. Some, but never enough, were supplied directly from Germany, including the Krupp L3H-163 often used for signal equipment and the Krauss-Maffei KM m9 halftrack, most of which towed the 8. 8 cm anti-tank guns but could be pressed into service to move bombers about an airfield if necessary. However, these were never available in sufficient numbers and the Condor Legion commandeered

Above Left: Condor Legion Tank Badge

Above Right: Condor Legion Wound Badge in Silver

Below: From left to right—unknown, Adolf Galland, Werner Mölders. *TRH Pictures*

Above Right: Spanish ground crew carry German SC50 bombs. Behind them is 1.K/88's He 111 25 • 92. *via Austin Brown Photo Library*

Right: Typical flight gear for Legion pilots. Note Adolf Galland in sunglasses in deck chair at right. *TRH Pictures*

Above: German Condor Legion Honour Cross for Next of Kin. This award was established the same day as the Spanish Cross to commemorate those legionaries who fell during the Spanish conflict. The award was a smaller version of the Spanish Cross with swords and it was produced from bronze or brass with a bronze wash. The award was presented to the next of kin in cases of soldiers killed or missing in action or if death occurred due to war related sickness. A total of 315 Honour Crosses were awarded.

Far Right: At a special ceremony held in the Marble Galley of the new Reich Chancellery Hitler, accompanied by Göring, presented the Spanish Cross in gold with diamonds to Air Force officers of the Legion Condor and naval officers from the pocket battleship *Deutschland*. Berlin, 6 June 1939. *via Brian L. Davies*

Top Left: Spanish Cross in Bronze With Swords. To obtain the Cross with Swords an individual had to be involved in front line combat, and the degree of experience and rank determined whether the Cross was bestowed in Bronze, Silver or Gold.

Above Left: Spanish Cross in Silver Without Swords.

Left: Spanish Cross in Gold With Swords. This was restricted to those who not only engaged the enemy, but had also excelled in the form of personal bravery or achievement. The highest grade, Gold with Diamonds, was strictly presented to those with the highest achievements or leadership in action. It was only awarded 28 times, with the majority going to Luftwaffe pilots.

civilian cars and trucks, used vehicles abandoned by the Republicans, or what could be scrounged from the Nationalists to transport personnel. Estimates suggest that the Condor Legion had a pool of some 1,500 vehicles of around 100 different types—a situation that proved a nightmare for maintenance personnel—and because of the poor condition of Spanish roads and frequent accidents, it was not unusual for up to 50 percent to be out of action at any one time. Because of these problems, the Condor Legion took to moving key personnel around on a specially configured train known as a *Wohnzug* (railway caravan). Typically, a *Wohnzug* consisted of nine carriages, a third of which contained sleeping compartments, and two locomotives.

Awards granted to Condor Legion personnel

Award	Date instituted	Recipients
Spanish Cross (1)	14 April 1939	
Gold with Swords and Diamonds		28
Gold with Swords		1,126
Silver with Swords		8,304
Silver without Swords		327
Bronze with Swords		8,462
Bronze without Swords		7,869
Cross of Honour for Relatives of the Dead	14 April 1939	315
Wound Badge (2)	22 May 1939	183
Tank Combat Badge (3)	10 July 1939	415

1) The six grades of the Spanish Cross were granted on the basis of the following criteria: Gold with Swords and Diamonds for repeated acts above and beyond the call of duty; Gold with Swords as for with Diamonds or for performing above and beyond the call of duty; Silver with Swords for taking part in several engagements; Silver without Swords as with Swords or for performing above and beyond the call of duty; Bronze with Swords for taking part in combat; and Bronze without Swords for three months of service in Spain.

2) The Wound Badge was granted in three classes—Gold, Silver and Black—to those wounded in the line of duty while serving in Spain.

3) The Tank Combat Badge of the Condor Legion was awarded to crews serving in Spain and came in both cloth and silver metal versions. Wilhelm Ritter von Thoma was presented with a unique gold version by his armoured units during the Nationalist victory parade through Madrid on 19 May 1939.

CONDOR LEGION AIRCRAFT MARKINGS

With only a very few exceptions involving the unofficial and temporary addition of the swastika, all of the German aircraft serving in the civil war had any emblems that linked them to Nazi Germany and the Luftwaffe removed before entering service at the front with the Condor Legion. Various new identification markings were added and these ranged from officially sanctioned designs to wholly unofficial devices chosen by individual pilots. The most common emblem found on Condor Legion aircraft was the cross motif that was applied to all Nationalist aircraft. This was generally found on the upper and lower surfaces of the wings close to the tips and on the tail rudder. In the former case it consisted of a white diagonal cross on a black roundel and in the latter position it appeared in reverse—a black diagonal cross on a white background. The second official emblem appeared towards the rear of the fuselage on both sides just forward of the tailplane. Initially, the device consisted of a black roundel behind which appeared two numerals divided by a small dash but the dash was subsequently deleted and its position taken by the black roundel. The one- or two-figure numeral applied in front of the roundel indicated the individual type of aircraft while the numeral behind effectively indicated the delivery number of the aircraft. With regard to the Condor Legion, in the former case number 2 indicated a Heinkel He 51, 6 a Messerschmitt Bf 109, 25 a Heinkel He 111, and 27 a Dornier Do 17, for example. In the latter case, the greater the number the later the delivery.

Apart from these markings, most if not all of the Condor Legion's various Staffeln had their own individual recognition emblems that were usually painted on the fuselage below the cockpit. In the case of J/88, its 1. Staffel aircraft carried a rendition of a marabou stork; 2. Staffel a black top hat; 3. Staffel various profiles of Mickey Mouse; and 4. Staffel the *Pik-As* (Ace of Clubs) in black on a white four-sided diamond with curved edges mounted on the black fuselage roundels. K/88's bombers showed slightly less variation—two of the Staffeln were identified by variants of an eagle carrying a bomb in its talons, both rendered in white, while a third made use of a pair of stylised wings and a bomb. Among the reconnaissance Staffeln A/88 aircraft could be identified by the head of a bearded devil, while AS/88 aircraft carried the Ace of Spades playing card on a black roundel.

The least official emblems seen were those produced for individual pilots or crews. These came in a variety of types from simple lettering to artworks of varying quality, or a mix of the two. Fighter pilots in particular flew aircraft decorated with nose art. Hannes Trautloft's aircraft was recognisable by a green heart painted immediately behind the cockpit and Adolf Galland's Heinkel He 51 was decorated with a white Maltese Cross positioned on the black fuselage roundels, which were edged in white. Gotthard Handrick's Bf 109 had a white propeller spinner painted on one side with the five-ringed symbol of the Olympic Games beneath which was the year 1936 and a laurel wreath, and on the opposite side the same symbol but with the date 1940 and a question mark. To leave no one in doubt as to who was flying his fighter, Handrick, who had won a gold medal in the 1936 Olympics in Berlin, also added a letter h in gothic script to the black fuselage roundels. As pilots and crew rotated home but their aircraft remained in Spain, it was not unusual for their nose art to undergo modification. Walter Grabmann, who took over Handrick's Bf 109 had the gothic script removed and replaced with an Arabic letter G for his own surname.

Above: He 111 tail surfaces being cleaned: note Legion X marking and K/88 eagle with bombs. *via Austin Brown Photo Library*

Opposite, Above: Do 17 27 • 28 — the first P model in Spain; seen at Bunuel with A/88 in late 1938. *via Austin Brown Photo Library*

Opposite, Centre: Fi 156 46 • 2 painted in dark grey upper surfaces/light grey lower. *via Chris Ellis*

Opposite, Below: Bf109Ds with SC-50s in the foreground. *TRH Pictures*

Above: Typical Bf 109 markings during the war. Note fin cross, wing markings and typical fuselage markings (in this case of 6 • 56 with top hat signifying 2.J/88).

Below: A Legion Condor Spanish Auxiliary's armband.

Left: The volunteers receive a rapturous reception from the people of Hamburg. *via Brian L. Davies*

Below: Hamburg, 31 May 1939. The presentation to members of the Legion of the newly instituted Spanish Cross (*Spanienkreuz*) in one of four classes, bronze, silver, gold and gold with diamonds, although these two classes of this Cross were held over for the special investiture to be held in Berlin on 6 June, see photo on page 77. All volunteers from the Civil War were to receive one of the four classes. It was also announced that the Legion Condor was to be officially dissolved within a few days of this ceremony and that in proud memory of the Legion the title 'Condor' had been bestowed by Adolf Hitler on a Luftwaffe squadron, an anti-aircraft artillery regiment and a signals battalion. *via Brian L. Davies*

PEOPLE

MÖLDERS, WERNER (1913–41)

Above: Oberst Werner Mölders. *TRH Pictures*

Mölders was born in Gelsenkirchen and joined the army in 1931, but after three years he requested a transfer to the Luftwaffe. He was initially designated unfit for flying but nevertheless successfully reapplied and was posted to a fighter unit. After serving with various squadrons he transferred to a training formation at Wiesbaden in April 1936 and two years later volunteered for the Condor Legion. Arriving in Spain on 14 April, he took command of 3./J/88 and quickly gained a reputation as a skilled pilot and able tactician. Between 15 July and 3 November Mölders shot down 14 Republican aircraft, most while flying a Bf 109C nicknamed *Luchs* (Lynx). While in Spain he was also partly responsible for developing the finger four or fan flying formation that became standard with the Luftwaffe's fighter units during World War 2.

Mölders left Spain at the end of 1938 as the highest scoring German ace of the conflict and went on to serve with JG 53 during the invasion of France and the Low Countries. Although his tally of kills continued to rise, he was shot down over France on 5 June 1940, and held prisoner for two weeks until the armistice secured his freedom. He was then given command of JG 51 but was shot down by an RAF Spitfire on 28 July and spent a month recovering from leg wounds. Returning to action during the Battle of Britain, he became the first German pilot to record 50 kills after shooting down three Hurricanes on 22 October.

Mölders continued to serve in the west until May 1941, by which time he had a score of 82 kills, and then took part in the invasion of Russia. On 30 June he overtook Baron Manfred von Richthofen as Germany's top ace of all time and on 15 July reached 100 aerial victories but then Göring ordered that he cease flying combat missions. Reward for his proven record as a pilot and his outstanding tactical skills came when Mölders was promoted to the rank of Generalmajor and made inspector-general of the Luftwaffe's fighter arm on 7 August. However, his potential in this role was never fully realised as he was killed in an air accident on 22 November. Flying in bad weather with low visibility, his Heinkel He 111 aircraft crashed into a chimney in Breslau as Mölders was making his way to Berlin from the Crimea to attend the state-sponsored public funeral of an equally renowned fighter pilot and senior Luftwaffe figure—Oberstgeneral Ernst Udet. Apart from winning the Spanish in Gold with Diamonds, Mölders had also received the Knight's Cross with Diamonds in part for destroying some 14 aircraft in Spain and a further 101 between 1939 and 1941.

OESAU, WALTER (1913–44)

Oesau began his military career by enlisting in the army during 1934 but within a year he was undergoing flight training and then served with the Jagdgeschwader Richthofen. He remained in Germany until April 1938, when he joined the Condor Legion in Spain and served as a fighter pilot with J/88. His first victory came on 15 July and by the end of the month his tally had risen to five kills. A further four victories were added between August and November, after which Oesau returned to Germany as the Luftwaffe urgently needed a pool of experienced pilots as the crisis over Czechoslovakia developed. During his time in Spain, Oesau, the Legion's fifth-equal most successful ace, had been wounded in action for which he received the Spanish Wound Badge, and was later awarded the Spanish Cross in Gold with Diamonds. After a spell with JG 2 he joined JG 51 in July 1939 and won his first victory of World War 2 on 13 May 1940. Oesau remained with JG 51 until November, by which time his total tally had reached 48 aircraft, a score including several occasions when he shot down two or more aircraft in a day during the Battle of Britain, and he was awarded the Knight's Cross.

Oesau transferred to JG 3, winning the Knight's Cross with Oak Leaves on 5 February 1941, and led the group during the invasion of the Soviet Union. Numerous aerial victories followed in quick succession, taking his total to 50 on 16 May, 70 on 8 July and 90 on 22 July. Awarded the Knight's Cross with Oak Leaves and Swords, Oesau moved to the west and then took command of JG 2, notching up his 100th kill on 12 August. Subsequently deemed too valuable to risk in further combat, he was given numerous staff appointments but on 12 November, 1943, he returned to action as commander of JG 1. Thrown into defending the Reich against the Allied strategic bombing offensive, Oesau scored 14 further victories but was killed when attacked by a P-38 Mustang over Belgium on 11 May 1944. His final score was 127 kills in 300 combat sorties, including nine in Spain, 74 on the Western Front and 44 on the Eastern Front.

Condor Legion Aces (1)

Name	Victories
Mölders, Werner	14
Schellmann, Wolfgang	12
Harder, Harro	11
Boddem, Peter	10
Bertram, Otto	9
Ensslen, Wilhelm	9
Ihlefeld, Herbert	9
Oesau, Walter	9
Seiler, Reinhard	9
Knüppel, Herwig	8
Mayer, Hans-Karl	8
Eberhardt, Kraft	7
Grabmann, Walter	7
Tietzen, Horst	7
Balthasar, Wilhelm	6
Pingel, Rolf	6
Rochel, Kurt	6
Schob, Herbert	6
Braunshim, Georg	5
Handrick, Gotthard	5
Houwald, Otto Heinrich von	5
Lippert, Wolfgang	5
Lützow, Günther	5
Schlichting, Joachim	5
Szuggar, Willi	5
Trautloft, Hannes	5

1) Some 118 Condor Legion pilots were credited with downing one or more enemy aircraft during the Spanish Civil War but the above named 26 aces accounted for a little over 50 percent of their total victories. Of the remainder, 12 pilots scored four victories, 20 scored three, 15 scored two and 45 scored one. Many went on to have further victories during World War 2 but none of the top four aces survived the conflict. Mölders was killed in a flying accident on 11 November 1941, Schellmann was probably killed after capture on the Eastern Front on 22, June 1941, Harder was shot down on 12 August 1940, while Boddem died in a flying accident on 20 March 1939. Several of the others were also killed between 1939 and 1945 including Ensslen, Oesau, Knüppel, Mayer, Tietzen, Pingel, Braunschim, Houwald and Lützow. Lippert died of wounds on 23 November 1941, while the more fortunate Schlichting was captured on 6 September 1940.

FREIHERR VON RICHTHOFEN, WOLFRAM (1895–1945)

Above: Wolfram Von Richthofen while commanding 2 Luftflotte. *TRH Pictures*

Born in Barzdorf, Silesia, on 10 October 1895 Richthofen was a cousin of the famous World War 1 ace Baron Manfred von Richthofen and in 1918 served in the squadron that had been named after his legendary relative. After Germany's defeat in World War 1 he studied engineering and then joined the much diminished Reichswehr, where he participated in several flying competitions. Between 1929 and 1933 he travelled to Italy as a member of the German General Staff. Returning to Germany he was attached to the Technical Division of the air ministry but in 1936 was appointed chief-of-staff of the Condor Legion for service in Spain. After serving in this capacity under Hugo Sperrle and Helmuth Volkmann, Richthofen took command of the Condor Legion in November 1938. During his time in Spain he shown excellent diplomatic skill in dealing with the Nationalist command and was also largely responsible for developing air tactics that would become standard within the Luftwaffe during World War 2, particularly in the field of ground-attack techniques. He returned home in May 1939 and served with Stuka units during the invasion of Poland in September and the Blitzkrieg against France and the Low Countries in May 1940. During July he was given command of Fliegerkorps VIII, a specialist unit of Stukas and reconnaissance aircraft that suffered severe losses during the Battle of Britain. In 1941 he gained the Knight's Cross with Oak Leaves and was made General der Flieger. During this period he served on the Eastern Front and was made a Generalfeldmarschall in February 1943. As head of Luftflotte IV he was privy to the preparations for the Kursk offensive but did not take part in the attack as he transferred to Italy to take command of Luftflotte II shortly before the battle opened. Von Richthofen died on 12 July 1945, after being diagnosed with an inoperable brain tumour.

SPERRLE, HUGO (1885–1953)

Sperrle, the son of a brewer, was born in Ludwigsburg and joined the German Army before World War 1. On the outbreak of the conflict he transferred to the air force and in 1919 served with an air detachment of the right-wing Freikorps. In 1925 he was attached to the Reichswehr Ministry and then held various regimental commands between 1929 and 1933. Once Hitler had assumed power that year Sperrle was transferred to the emerging Luftwaffe and in 1934 was promoted to the rank of

Generalmajor. Two years later Hermann Göring ordered him to take command of the Condor Legion and Sperrle held the position until late October 1937. For his work in Spain he was promoted to the rank of General der Flieger in November 1937 and then took charge of what was to become Luftflotte III, which was stationed around Munich in southern Germany along the Austrian border. Luftflotte III did not take part in the invasion of Poland in September 1939 but played a prominent role in support of Gerd von Rundstedt's Army Group A during the invasion of France the following year. Sperrle won the Knight's Cross in May and was promoted to Generalfeldmarschall in June, and his air group next played the leading role in the Battle of Britain. As the Luftwaffe's offensive stalled, Sperrle correctly but unsuccessfully continued to argue that it had to keep attacking RAF airfields rather than targeting London, which had become the new priority.

By May 1941 Luftflotte III was much reduced in strength as units were sent east for the invasion of the Soviet Union and Sperrle, who remained at his headquarters at the Palais du Luxembourg in Paris, came under considerable criticism for his laxness. Goebbels accused him of living a life of unrestrained hedonism and Albert Speer remarked that his 'craving for luxury and public display ran a close second to that of his superior Göring; he was also his match in corpulence'. Hitler considered dismissing him but Sperrle held on to his job for the next three years and was chiefly responsible for defending Belgium, France and the Low Countries from the Allied strategic air offensive. By D-Day his command was so reduced and his own abilities so compromised by his lifestyle that he was unable to offer any effective opposition to the landings. His inactivity over the following weeks sealed his fate. Sperrle was dismissed in August and never re-employed. After the defeat of Germany he was tried but acquitted on all charges of war crimes at Nuremberg and subsequently died in Munich on 7 April 1953.

Above: Generalfeldmarschall Hugo Sperrle seen when leading Luftflotte 3 in 1940. *TRH Pictures*

RITTER VON THOMA, WILHELM JOSEF (1891–1948)

During World War 1 von Thoma served in some of the fiercest battles on both the Eastern and Western Front as well as in Serbia. He was wounded four times and received numerous awards before being captured by US troops on 18 July 1918. In the interwar period he remained in the much-reduced army, holding various commands in the regular

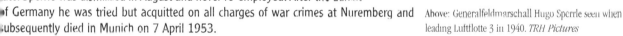

Senior Officers of the Condor Legion

Name	Rank	Dates
Sperrle, Hugo (1)	Generalmajor	November 1936–October 1937
Volkmann, Helmuth (2)	Generalmajor	October 1937–November 1938
Plocher, Hermann (3)	Major	November 1938
Richthofen, Wolfram Freiherr von	Generalmajor	November 1938–June 1939

1) Transferred from Spain to command Luftflotte III.
2) Volkmann served with the German Army from 1907 onwards but transferred to the Luftwaffe in the mid-1930s. After a spell as head of its War Academy following command of the Condor Legion, he returned to the regular army but was killed in a car accident on 21 August 1940.
3) Temporary appointment between departure of Volkmann and arrival of von Richthofen.

Above: Ritter Wilhelm von Thoma.

infantry. In July 1922 he transferred to the 7th (Bavarian) Motorised Battalion, thereby beginning his career in mobile warfare, and 12 years later he joined the *Kraftfahr-Lehrkommando* (Motorised Demonstration Command) at Ohrdorf, Germany's first out-and-out tank unit that von Thoma later described as 'the grandmother of all the others'. In October 1935, when Germany formally announced the establishment of its first three armoured divisions, von Thoma was given command of the 4th Panzer Regiment, part of Oberst Heinz Guderian's 2nd Panzer Division. On 23 September 1936, von Thoma was given command of the German ground force contingent in Spain. He arrived in Spain and began training Nationalist troops in tank warfare, infantry tactics, artillery procedures and signalling. Although von Thoma was supposedly to act only as an advisor and oversee various support programmes, he made frequent forays to the front, later claiming that he had taken part in some 192 tank combats during the civil war. For his leadership in the conflict von Thoma received various awards, including the Spanish Cross in Gold with Swords and Diamonds, the Spanish Military Medal with Diamonds, the Spanish Campaign Medal and the Condor Legion Tank Combat Badge.

With the outbreak of World War 2, von Thoma took part in the Blitzkrieg against Poland in September 1939, serving with the 2nd Panzer Division's 3rd Panzer Regiment. After taking command of the latter unit from mid-September to early March 1940, he undertook senior administrative duties relating to Germany's armoured forces but was then placed in temporary command of the 17th Panzer Division on the Eastern Front on 17 July 1941. He later commanded the 20th Panzer Division in the same theatre until early July 1942 and then, after a brief spell on the general staff, moved to North Africa to command the Afrika Korps in September. Von Thoma relinquished this position in late October after Generalfeldmarschall Erwin Rommel returned from sick leave on the 25th and took charge of Panzer Army Afrika. This force was soon pitched into the Second Battle of Alamein, which saw the German forces bled white by the British. Von Thoma was captured by the British at Tel el Mampsra, west of El Alamein on 4 November, after being forced to abandon his burning tank during a fierce fight. From 1942 until 1946 he was a prisoner-of-war in various British camps and then returned to Bavaria, where he remained until his death.

Right: Eduard Milch, German Secretary of State for Air, organised the German involvement in Spain. Chairman of Lufthansa from June 1926, he used the company as a cover behind which he developed the manpower necessary for the Luftwaffe. In 1935, when the Luftwaffe was recognised, it already had 1,000 aircraft and 20,000 trained men — from whose numbers many of the Condor Legion would be drawn. Milch is seen here at Le Bourget on 4 October 1937. The aircraft in the background are Amiot 143s. *TRH Pictures*

ASSESSMENT

When assessing German involvement in Spain two questions are paramount: to what extent did it ensure Franco's ultimate victory and what impact did it have on the weapons and tactics that the Wehrmacht deployed during World War 2? In the first days of the civil war, from August to November 1936, when the Condor Legion proper was organised, the commitment was seen as short-term and limited in scale. Yet the score or so of Luftwaffe transports sent to Spain enabled Franco's Army of Africa to reach the Spanish mainland. Its arrival did not guarantee a Nationalist victory but probably ensured that the rebellion would survive the initial chaos that surrounded it. Subsequently, the German commitment grew massively in response to the foreign aid dispatched to the Republic— the Condor Legion was sent as were smaller numbers of army and naval personnel and vast quantities of supplies to fuel the Nationalist war effort. German ground, sea and air forces undertook combat missions but the value of the training they gave to the Nationalists, although less glamorous, was probably of equal if not greater value. Equally noteworthy was the contribution of the German officers who joined Franco's staff. After the failure to take Madrid in late 1936 and early 1937 they convinced him to nibble away successively at Republican territory—a strategy that prolonged the war but probably made victory more likely—and also played significant roles in the direction of the battles that followed the stalemate around the capital.

German military personnel undoubtedly played a major part in developing the skills of Franco's forces. The Condor Legion established various schools where Nationalists were taught anti-aircraft, aircraft maintenance, signals and flying techniques. In all, some 500 Spanish aircrew received flight instruction, while a further 60 or so were trained in Germany. On the ground, Gruppe Imker contained probably no more than 600 Germans but a network of bases was established across Spain to train Nationalist recruits in various military skills. These included officer schools, non-commissioned officer facilities and an infantry training school. Of equal importance were facilities where other German instructors taught artillery, mortar, and chemical warfare and signal techniques. Armour and anti-tank training was also undertaken near Madrid and Toledo, where recruits were taught on both German and captured Soviet tanks. Reports suggest that some 56,000 Nationalists soldiers were schooled by the various German detachments, thereby providing Franco with a large corps of well-trained and technically proficient soldiers. The North Sea Group, although the smallest of Germany's detachments, trained Nationalists in the use of torpedo-boats, communications and seamanship but the naval campaign during the civil war was of comparatively minor importance.

The Condor Legion played a major part spearheading many Nationalist victories. Its chief responsibilities were to gain air superiority, interdict the flow of supplies to the front, and support ground offensives—all roles that were successfully accomplished in Spain. By operating in these ways in Spain, the Legion undoubtedly gave the Nationalists air superiority over many battlefields from 1937 and eventually over all Spain. Its fighter

Winners of the Spanish Cross in Gold with Swords and Diamonds

Name	Rank	Unit
Balthasar, Wilhelm	Oberleutnant	J/88
Bertram, Otto	Oberleutnant	J/88
Boddem, Peter (1)	Leutnant	J/88
Eberhardt, Kraft (2)	Oberleutnant	J/88
Ensslen, Wilhelm	Oberleutnant	J/88
Fehlhaber, Paul (3)	Leutnant	LN/88
Galland, Adolf	Oberleutnant	J/88
Harder, Harro	Hauptmann	J/88
Harlinghausen, Martin	Major	AS/88
Henrici, Oskar (2)	Leutnant	J/88
Graf Hoyos, Max	Oberleutnant	K/88
Kessel, Hans-Detlef von (4)	Oberleutnant	A/88
Lützow, Günther	Hauptmann	J/88
Mehnert, Karl	Oberstleutnant	K/88
Mölders, Werner	Hauptmann	J/88
Freiherr von Moreau, Rudolf (5)	Hauptmann	K/88
Neudörffer, Wolfgang	Hauptmann	K/88
Oesau, Walter	Oberleutnant	J/88
Freiherr von Richthofen, Wolfram	Generalmajor	S/88
Runze, Heinz (6)	Leutnant	A/88
Schellmann, Wolfgang	Hauptmann	J/88
Schlichting, Joachim	Hauptmann	J/88
Seiler, Reinhard	Oberleutnant	J/88
Sperrle, Hugo	General der Flieger	S/88
Stärcke, Bernhard	Oberleutnant	K/88
Thoma, Wilhelm Josef von	Oberst	Panzerabteilung Imker
Volkmann, Helmut	General der Flieger	S/88
Wolff, Karl-Heinz	Major	AS/88

1) Awarded posthumously after his death in a flying accident on 20 March 1939.
2) Awarded posthumously after both were shot down and killed over Madrid on 13 November 1936.
3) Awarded posthumously after being killed by enemy artillery fire near Bilbao on 11 June 1937.
4) Awarded posthumously after he was shot down by anti-aircraft fire near Llanes on 4 September 1937.
5) Awarded posthumously after his death while at the controls of the new Junkers Ju 88 at Rechlin test centre in Germany on 4 April 1939.
6) Awarded posthumously after Runze was killed by anti-aircraft fire over Teruel on 1 January 1938.

pilots scored a little more than 300 confirmed kills, a not insignificant contribution to the battle for air superiority but one actually dwarfed by the Italians, who claimed 903, and one nearly matched by the Nationalists, who recorded 294 aerial victories.

The Legion's K/88 bombers dropped some 21,000 tons of ordnance and the German pilots claimed to have sunk 60 vessels of all types. It is also clear that German instructors from Imker and Drohne were sent to the front and engaged in combat but the paucity of adequate armour on both sides meant that tanks never had more than localised significance in combat. Although used against Republican aircraft with success, being credited with 61 enemy aircraft shot down, the heavy 8.8 cm Flak batteries also performed well in support of Nationalist ground attacks and in the anti-tank role.

Spain confirmed Germany's faith in the evolving concept of Blitzkrieg that was based on the close co-operation between ground and air units but also effectively subordinated the latter to the needs of the former. Tactically, the Luftwaffe drew several lessons from the civil war that for good or bad influenced its performance during World War 2. Werner Mölders developed the highly effective *Rotte* and *Schwarm*, loose two and four-aircraft

Below: Adolf Galland. *TRH Pictures*

formations of fighters that allowed them to fly at faster speeds and gave greater flexibility and manoeuvrability in combat. Germany's medium bombers proved inaccurate when attacking pinpoint targets, but this failure was seemingly offset by the success of the ground-attack and dive-bombing tactics developed by Wolfram von Richthofen. Losses of ground-attack aircraft and bombers were comparatively low because the Condor Legion had effectively gained the air superiority that allowed these types to operate at will over mostly short ranges with often little or no fighter escort. Luftwaffe strategists recognised to some degree that these circumstances might not apply in the future and partly addressed the potential problems by developing faster, more heavily armed bombers, boosting the firepower of the Bf 109 by adding a cannon, developing a long-range fighter, the Messerschmitt Bf 110, and giving generally greater emphasis to fighter production. Yet, as the Battle of Britain showed, the Luftwaffe's experiences in Spain did not prepare it to meet and defeat independently at long range an enemy equipped with modern fighters.

Spain was also something of a proving ground for Germany's untried tanks and evolving armoured tactics. Although the number of tanks in action was comparatively small and they saw limited service, several conclusions were reached that aided the

Chiefs-of-Staff of the Condor Legion

Name	Rank	Dates
Alexander Holle	Major	November 1936–January 1937
Richthofen, Wolfram Freiherr von (1)	Oberstleutnant	January 1937–January 1938
Plocher, Hermann	Major	January 1938–November 1938
Seidemann, Hans	Oberstleutnant	November 1938–June 1939

1) Following disagreements with Volkmann, who resented his influence with the Nationalist leadership and clear understanding of the air war, von Richthofen requested and was granted leave to return to Germany on 11 January.

development of Blitzkrieg. A key moment came in early January 1937 when a Nationalist assault on Madrid led by German tanks was easily repulsed by Republican anti-tank guns.

Many foreign observers argued that tanks were far too easily destroyed by anti-tank guns and could only operate successfully in the infantry support role as a type of mobile artillery rather than as the spearhead of an offensive. Von Thoma and others drew different conclusions from the Madrid battle. They argued that the tanks had fought in much smaller numbers than appropriate for a leading role and that motorised infantry and anti-tank guns able to keep up with the armour and close air support to neutralise the enemy artillery were vital.

Finally, the PzKpfw I tanks, never seen as more than an interim design for training Germany's own armoured corps, were clearly too thinly armoured, under-gunned and under-powered to survive on the battlefield. Consequently, added emphasis was given to newer designs that overcame these weaknesses, although few were available for the Blitzkriegs of 1939 and 1940.

PARADEMARSCH DER LEGION CONDOR

Wir zogen übers weite Meer
Ins fremde Spanierland
Zu kämpfen für der Freiheit Ehr
Weil haß und Krieg entbrannt
Hier herrschten Marxisten und Roten
Der Pöbel der hatte die Macht
Da hat, als der Ordnung Boten
Der Deutsche Hilfe gebracht.

Wir jagten sie wie eine Herde
Und der Teufel, der lachte dazu
Ha ha ha ha ha!
Die Roten in spanischer Luft
Und zur Erde
Wir ließen sie nirgends in Ruh.

Hat auch der Tod mit harter Hand
Die Besten oft gefällt
Wir hielten aus, der Wall stand fest
Die rote Flut zerschellt
Und ziehen die Legionäre
Als Sieger ins deutsche Land
Dann schreiten mit unsere Toten
Wir heben zum Gruße die Hand.

Wir jagten sie wie eine Herde...

DIE LEGION CONDOR

Wir flogen jenseits der Grenzen
Mit Bomben gegen den Feind
Hoch über der spanischen Erde
Mit den Fliegern Italiens vereint.

Wir sind deutsche Legionäre
Die Bombenflieger der Legion
Im Kampf um Freiheit und um Ehre
Soldaten der Nation
Vorwärts, Legionäre!

Vorwärts im Kampf
Sind wir nicht allein
Und die Freiheit muß
Ziel unseres Kampfes sein
Vorwärts, Legionäre!

Die Roten, die wurden geschlagen
Im Angriff bei Tag und bei Nacht
Die Fahne zum Siege getragen
Und dem Volke der Friede gebracht.

Wir sind deutsche Legionäre...

REFERENCE

Partly because of the official cloak of secrecy that surrounded the deployment of German forces to Spain between 1936 and 1939, the material readily available on certain aspects of the intervention is extremely sparse, although there was almost a flood of officially backed celebratory books published in Nazi Germany shortly after the end of the Spanish Civil War. Most aspects of the actual Condor Legion's involvement in the air war have been covered in considerable detail by modern authors but there is far less information available on the ground and naval units that were committed to the conflict. In the latter cases many of the sources simply rehash and repeat what little is already known. As a general rule the story of Germany's involvement in Spain is not particularly well served by internet sites and a considerable number are too brief, poorly written and lacking any great insight.

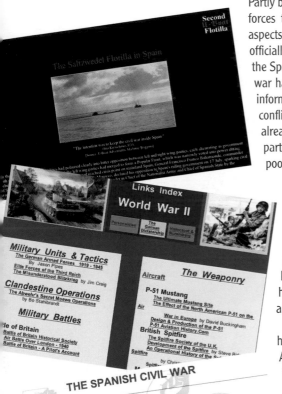

WEBSITES

http://www.ihr.org/jhr/v07/v07p133 Oppenheimer.html
An interesting site that includes an extensive analytical account of the lessons learned by the Luftwaffe from the experiences of the Condor Legion in Spain and how they not only influenced events in Poland and France during 1939–40 but also related to aircraft types and military doctrines.

http://www.vanguardnetwork.com/germans.htm
A site containing various speeches given by leading figures of the Nazi regime, including one by Hitler to returning members of the Condor Legion in Berlin's Lustgarden on 6 June 1939.

http://www.uboatwar.net/spain.htm
Part of a site dedicated to Nazi Germany's U-boat arm that includes details of the secret operations conducted by submarines of the 2nd U-boat Flotilla in the waters off Spain and naval winners of the Spanish Cross.

http://www.eliteforces.freewire.co.uk/index.htm
A site dedicated to the various elite units of the Third Reich, including the Condor Legion. While some sections on the latter are adequate, such as those on uniforms and insignia, ground forces and background, others are either limited or uncompleted.

http://www.wehrmacht-awards.com/
A site specialising in the insignia and badges of the Third Reich. It also covers several of those awarded to the Condor Legion, including the Spanish Cross of Honour, Spanish cuff title and the Honour Cross for Next of Kin. Each entry comprises details of the insignia, award criteria and photographs of winners.

http://users.accesscom.m.ca/magnusfamily/scwger.htm
An alphabetically arranged list of pilots from J/88 who scored one or more kills with the Condor Legion during their tours of duty in Spain.

http://www.submarinos.net/hojas/liali.html
Coverage of the background to the deployment of German naval vessels to Spain and brief details of their participation, notably Operation 'Ursula' and the Republican bombing of the Deutschland in May 1937.

http://www.feldgrau.com/deutsch-lutz.html
A bare-bones history of the Panzerschiff Deutschland that includes short entries on its numerous patrols in Spanish waters. The site also contains a photograph of the memorial to those of the ship's crew killed by Republican bombers in late May 1937.

BIBLIOGRAPHY

Baker, David: *Adolf Galland—The Authorised Biography*; Windrow and Greene, London, 1996.
The author covers the whole of Galland's life and distinguished military career, dedicating roughly one and a half chapters to his time serving in and commanding 3./J/88 during the Spanish Civil War.

Beevor, Antony: *The Spanish Civil War*; Orbis Publishing Limited, London, 1982.
An early work by the highly successful author of monumental studies of the Battles of Stalingrad and Berlin, this volume covers the political and military aspects of the civil war. Apart from useful maps, it also contains a chronology of events, thumbnail sketches of the numerous political parties and an extensive bibliography.

Bender, Roger James and Law, Richard D.: *Uniforms, Organisation and History of the Legion Condor*; R. James Bender Publishing, San Jose, California, 1973.
A volume containing a large number of photographs that covers most aspects of the Condor Legion during its time in Spain.

Elstob, Peter: *Condor Legion*; Ballantine Books, New York, 1973.
An overview of the Luftwaffe's commitment to the Spanish Civil War that is profusely illustrated but is somewhat let down by the text.

Galland, Adolf: *The First and the Last*; Methuen, London, 1955.
The memoirs of one of the most successful Luftwaffe pilots of World War 2, this volume also details his experiences flying a Heinkel He 51 dive-bomber in ground-support missions during the Spanish Civil War.

Howson, Gerald: *Aircraft of the Spanish Civil War, 1936-1939*; Putnam Aeronautical Books, 2003.

A monumental work that covers the 280 or so types of aircraft that saw service on both sides during the conflict.

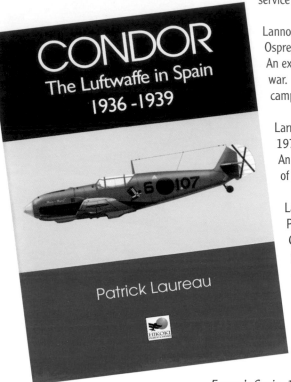

Lannon, Frances: Essential Histories 37: *The Spanish Civil War, 1936-1939*; Osprey Publishing Limited, London, 2002.
An excellent introduction to the causes, course and consequences of the civil war. Its also includes numerous photographs and a series of battle and campaign maps.

Larrazabel, Jésus Salas: *Air War over Spain*; Ian Allan Publishing, London, 1974.
An overview of the battle for air supremacy over Spain, including details of Condor Legion operations.

Laureau, Patrick: *Condor—The Luftwaffe in Spain, 1936-1939*; Hikoki Publications, 2001.
Containing some 70,000 words and some 450 black-and-white photographs, this is an exhaustive study of the Condor Legion. The author outlines Operation '*Feuerzauber*' and then details the Legion's organisation, while subsequent sections deal with its various units and the aircraft they contained. Information on which aircraft took part in the campaign, exhaustive work on serial numbers and pilots made this book invaluable when producing the captions for this book!

Leitz, Christian: *Economic Relations between Nazi Germany and Franco's Spain, 1936-1945*; Oxford University Press, 1996.
Although the bulk of the book covers the period of World War 2, there are two chapters that dwell on the civil war. In the first the author reviews the importance of HISMA and ROWAK, the agencies created to oversee the flow of Nazi aid to the Nationalists, while the second covers Anglo-German economic rivalry in Spain and the Montana project, the scheme designed to guarantee Germany bulk supplies of the various outputs from Spanish mines.

Mitchell Jr., Samuel W.: *Eagles of the Third Reich: The Men Who Made the Luftwaffe*; Presidio Press, Novato, California, 1997.
A useful volume that offers biographies of the leading figures in the development of the Luftwaffe. Several of the entries are of interest to students of the Condor Legion, including Adolf Galland, Hermann Göring, Werner Mölders, Wolfram von Richthofen and Hugo Sperrle.

Proctor, Raymond L.: *Hitler's Luftwaffe in the Spanish Civil War*; Greenwood Press, Westport, Connecticut, 1983.
An extensive history of the origins of the Condor Legion. Apart from analysing the Legion's difficulties encountered in fighting in a foreign land, the author also looks at its role in several critical battles. Much of his research is based on Spanish and German documents and interviews with former members of the Legion.

Shores, Christopher: *Osprey Airwar 3: Spanish Civil War Air Forces*; Osprey Publishing Limited, London, 1977.
A brief illustrated survey of the air conflict during the civil war that covers not only the Nationalist and Republican forces but also provides information on the Italian flying

contingent and the Condor Legion. It also contains a section of full-colour artworks of selected uniforms, aircraft and insignia.

Thomas, Gordon, and Morgan-Witts, Max: *The Day Guernica Died*; Hodder & Stoughton, London, 1975.
A study of one of the most infamous episodes of the Spanish Civil War and the Condor Legion's central role in the destruction of the Basque town in April 1937.

Thomas, Hugh: *The Spanish Civil War*; Eyre and Spotiswoode Publishers Limited, London, 1961.
This is one of the first, best and most definitive histories of the conflict. It may have been surpassed to some degree by more recent research but remains a vital starting point for anyone with more than a passing interest in the events of 1936–39.

Turnbull, Patrick: *Men-at-Arms 74: The Spanish Civil War, 1936-39*; Osprey Publishing Limited, London, 1977.
A short history of the conflict with individual chapters on its background, the Nationalist and Republican forces and its various campaigns. The volume also contains a section of colour plates of the various troops who fought for the rival sides.

MEMORIALS

Surviving photographs show that several memorials were erected in Spain between 1936 and 1939 to commemorate members of the Condor Legion killed while fighting in the civil war. The total number is unknown and how many survive to the present is problematical. They appear to have been built in a variety of styles, using different materials from concrete or dressed stone to slabs of rock. Some had the individual particulars engraved on a metal plaque, while others were carved directly onto the stone They carried the names of either a single individual or several of the dead and most appear to have various German inscriptions recording the fact that they died in the 'War for a Nationalist Spain' or 'For Germany and a free Nationalist Spain'. The Spanish Nationalists also took the trouble to rename several streets to honour members of the Condor Legion, although once again how many—if any—survive today is open to question. Back in Germany the Nazi authorities constructed a memorial to the 32 men who died on the *Deutschland* when it was attacked by Republican aircraft. It consisted of a simple rectangular plinth decorated with two eagles between which were inscribed the words 'To the dead of the *Panzerschiff Deutschland* who fell on 29 May 1938, at Ibiza'.

Below: Condor Legion memorial.

INDEX